FOR THE LOVE OF
BOOKS

A COMPANION

GRAHAM TARRANT

summersdale

FOR THE LOVE OF BOOKS

An Hachette UK Company
www.hachette.co.uk

Summersdale Publishers Ltd
Part of Octopus Publishing Group Limited
Carmelite House
50 Victoria Embankment
LONDON
EC4Y 0DZ
UK

www.summersdale.com

Printed and bound in the Czech Republic

ISBN: 978-1-78685-270-0

Substantial discounts on bulk quantities of Summersdale books are available to corporations, professional associations and other organisations. For details contact general enquiries: telephone: +44 (0) 1243 771107 or email: enquiries@summersdale.com.

For Abigail, Francesca and Rose.
And for Ricardo Oliveira Costa.

CONTENTS

INTRODUCTION

Books are companions for life – and ideal companions at that. They are constantly there when you need them, uncomplaining if cast aside, always ready to continue the relationship wherever it left off. You can take a book (paper or screen) on a plane or train, to the beach or to a hospital appointment. Sitting alone in a cafe or restaurant becomes a less solitary experience if you are accompanied by a book.

Books, at their best, can nourish the mind and liberate the spirit. They can comfort, humour, thrill, intrigue and arouse. Reading can be a leisurely affair, allowing time for reflection or to retrace one's steps in an intricate narrative. It can be a white-knuckle ride, pitching the reader, wide-eyed and dry-mouthed, into the on-rushing story. And few experiences are more rewarding than reading to children, especially a much-loved book from one's own early years.

It is hard to imagine a world without books, though some dystopian novels have painted a grim picture of such an eventuality. Even in the real world the decline, if not the actual demise, of the book has been confidently forecast from time to time. Cinema, television, video games, the internet and social media have all been cited as threats to its survival. Yet the latest market trends (in the UK at any rate) show the book to be in rude health, with sales of the traditional printed form more buoyant than those of the electronic upstart. To those of us with a love of books, this comes as no surprise.

Authors vary as much as the books they write, though they all share the daunting challenge of getting words on paper. Some have led lives as unlikely and remarkable as any work of fiction. Many have struggled with poverty, prejudice, addiction and the dreaded writer's block. Others have found it necessary (and financially fruitful) to channel their prolific outpourings through a pipework of pseudonyms.

This is a light-hearted book about books and the people who write them. It has stories, characters and plots, which are all the more compelling for being true. There are books and writers to discover, or perhaps to revisit. Readers with literary aspirations of their own can pick through the mixed experiences of those who have come before. All this and more will hopefully keep the pages turning. That is as much as any author can ask.

THE COMING OF
THE BOOK

Before the invention of writing, the spread of 'literature' was by word of mouth. Folk tales, legends and epic sagas were transmitted in spoken form, often by itinerant storytellers. Many were embellished over centuries. Some were later written down and are still read today, such as the Mesopotamian *Epic of Gilgamesh* (*c.*2000 BC), said to be the oldest story in existence, and the Greek sagas of *The Iliad* and *The Odyssey* (*c.*750 BC), attributed to the allegedly blind poet Homer but probably a combined effort involving other bards.

THE BOOK TAKES SHAPE

Writing is generally credited to the ancient civilisation of Sumer, later known as southern Mesopotamia, round about 3000 BC. The book began to take shape in many different ways.

The Sumerians themselves wrote on clay tablets, while in ancient China, the earliest forms were made from wood or bamboo leaves bound with cord. In Egypt and Greece, the written word was committed to papyrus scrolls, which were unrolled to reveal their contents. The Romans, in the first century AD, moved things on with the introduction of the codex: manuscripts of vellum or parchment, stacked sequentially and attached along one edge so that pages could be turned.

IT'S A FACT!

The word 'book' is derived from the Old English *bōc*, originally a document or charter. It is related to the Dutch *boek* and German *Buch*. Another associated word is 'beech', the wood on which ancient runes were often carved.

The Chinese chipped in with two seismic inventions, that of paper and printing. Paper suitable for writing purposes was first manufactured in AD 105. Woodblock printing (the characters and images carved onto wood before being inked and applied to paper) came a century or two later. The world's oldest-known printed book, *The Diamond Sutra* – a sacred Buddhist text, written in Chinese and dated AD 868 – was produced using this technique.

The next significant development, in the eleventh century and again courtesy of the Chinese, was the invention of moveable type. Instead of cumbersome wood-carving, printers used individual characters made from fired clay to create an image or body of text. As a result, books could be created faster and in greater quantities.

LIBRARY OF ALEXANDRIA

Founded in the third century BC and dedicated to the Muses (in Greek mythology, the nine goddesses of the arts), this was the most famous library in the ancient world. The legendary book depository was created by Ptolemy I Soter (*c*.367–282 BC), a former Macedonian general who became king of Egypt. For close to 300 years under the Ptolemaic Dynasty, Alexandria would be a centre of Greek culture.

The contents of the library consisted mainly of papyrus scrolls, several of which might comprise a single piece of work. Estimates of the total number of books housed vary between 400,000 and 700,000. Some of the works were original, others painstakingly copied by hand. The Greek philosopher Aristotle (384–322 BC) and the playwrights Aeschylus (524–456 BC), Sophocles (*c*.496–406 BC) and Euripides (480–406 BC) were among those whose works lined the shelves. The acquisition of books was relentless, and at almost any price. Ships entering the harbour were often searched, any books found on-board being confiscated for copying. If a book was of particular value or interest, the library would hang on to the original version and hand back a copy.

ILLUMINATED MANUSCRIPTS

Book production was a major activity in many European monasteries. Monks meticulously copied texts in the scriptorium (a spacious room set aside for the purpose), working only in daylight hours for fear of candles setting alight the manuscripts. Some texts would be embellished – illuminated – with illustrations or other decorative features, many of them amazingly detailed. Richly coloured illustrations of religious figures and symbols, and of flora and fauna, were augmented by intricately patterned borders. The illuminating effect was achieved by the delicate application of gold leaf or specks of gold, a process known as 'burnishing'. The earlier works were written on vellum or parchment, but by the Middle Ages paper was in general use.

The bound manuscripts produced by monasteries became models for the first printed books. Some became treasured works of art, such as the Lindisfarne Gospels (remarkably the creation of just one artist, Eadfrith, Bishop of Lindisfarne, between 698 and 721) which is now on display at the British Library in London. Eadfrith used a mixture of animal, vegetable and mineral pigments to achieve the exceptional range of colours on display, and there are clear influences of Anglo-Saxon jewellery and enamel work in the ornate lettering and decoration, making the Lindisfarne Gospels an important example of early English art. The eighth-century *Book of Kells*, another monastic masterpiece, is on permanent view at Trinity College, Dublin – though only one page a day, so you may want to make several visits. Its 680 pages (just sixty have gone missing over the years) are exquisitely decorated, justifying perhaps the sacrifice of the 185 calves whose skins produced the vellum on which the text is written and illustrated.

GUTENBERG'S BIBLE

Born in the German city of Mainz *c.*1398, Johannes Gutenberg was a man of many talents: blacksmith, goldsmith, diamond polisher, printer and publisher. Through his invention of moveable metal type, which was more durable and simpler to manipulate than either clay or woodblocks, he revolutionised the printing process in Europe. His most famous printed work is known as the Gutenberg Bible; also as the 'Forty-two Line Bible' because it has forty-two lines to the page; or the 'Mazarin Bible', having been discovered in Cardinal Mazarin's library in Paris in 1760. Whatever its name, the first printed edition of the Bible was published in 1455, though the work itself is undated. By this time, however, Gutenberg had fallen out with his financial partner Johann Fust and been forced out of the business, losing all claim to his magnificent creation.

The indefatigable Gutenberg set up another printing establishment, with the help of a new sponsor, and continued to publish books. Later he was ennobled by the Archbishop of Mainz in recognition of his remarkable achievements. By the end of the fifteenth century (thirty-two years after Gutenberg's death) it is estimated that some 35,000 separate editions of books had been printed. Many of these had religious, philosophical or scientific themes and were often written in Latin. Some resembled the illuminated manuscripts of the monasteries. All would help spread learning and the ideas of a new age.

IT'S A FACT!

The world's smallest printed book measures just 1mm square. The 12-page edition of the nursery rhyme *Old King Cole* was produced in Scotland in 1985 and has to be read under a microscope.

WILLIAM CAXTON

England's first printer was born in Kent *c.*1422. In his twenties, he moved to Bruges, in Belgium, where he lived for thirty years, becoming a successful dealer in textiles and governor of the flamboyantly named Company of Merchant Adventurers. In 1469, he changed career and embarked on a translation of a French text about the Trojan War, *Recuyell of the Historyes of Troye* (*A Collection of the Histories of Troy*), which would become the first book to be printed in the English language.

Having studied printing on a prolonged visit to Cologne, Caxton returned to England in 1476 and set up his own press at Westminster. Over the next fifteen years until his death in 1491, he produced around 90 books, among them Geoffrey Chaucer's *The Canterbury Tales* and Sir Thomas Malory's *Le Morte d'Arthur*. He translated (generally from French) many of the works himself, including the first English edition of *Aesop's Fables*.

POETIC PILGRIMAGE

The English poet Geoffrey Chaucer (*c.*1343–1400) is one of the greatest literary figures of the Middle Ages. A well-connected public servant, he worked in the king's service and was entrusted with several diplomatic missions abroad. As a writer, his most famous and ambitious work is *The Canterbury Tales*, which he began in 1387. A diverse group of thirty pilgrims assembles at the Tabard Inn at Southwark, before setting out for the shrine of St Thomas Beckett in Canterbury. To pass time on the journey, they engage in a storytelling contest.

Chaucer died before he could complete the work. As it stands, there is a general prologue and twenty-four tales, amounting to 17,000 lines of verse and prose. A character sketch introduces each storyteller, and the tales are as varied as the pilgrims themselves – from the courtly knight to the uncouth miller, from the prim prioress to the five-times-married wife of Bath. Together their stories provide a vivid and vastly entertaining portrait of medieval England.

PUBLISHERS LAUNCHED

Until the nineteenth century, printers, booksellers and sometimes authors themselves acted as the publishers of a book. The English novelist Samuel Richardson (1689–1761) was entirely self-sufficient in this regard; the proprietor of a thriving printing business in London, he wrote, printed and published two of the most successful novels of his time – *Pamela* (1740) and *Clarissa* (1748).

The Church and academic institutions both commissioned and purchased quantities of books, along with other publications, with the result that many printers and booksellers located their businesses close to universities and centres of religious study. Dealings with authors became a straightforward commercial transaction (though payment was often erratic and a matter of fierce dispute), replacing the earlier system of patronage in which writers were financially supported throughout their creative endeavours by a wealthy patron: Shakespeare's benefactor, for example, was the Earl of Southampton.

As the book market expanded, driven by the demands of a wider reading public, cheaper book production and better distribution, publishers came into their own as distinct from printers or booksellers. A new player in the game, the literary agent, emerged towards the end of the nineteenth century and would change the relationship between author and publisher. In 1926, the Book of the Month Club was launched in America and promptly spawned imitators on both sides of the Atlantic. With television not yet invented, and computers only the stuff of science fiction, the future seemed an open book.

As a young man, America's first president George Washington (1732–99) worked as a book salesman, once selling several hundred copies of a volume with the catchy title *The American Savage: How He May Be Tamed by the Weapons of Civilisation.*

LIBRARY MATTERS

There were many private collections of books from antiquity onwards, some housed in monasteries, others in stately homes or at the great universities. The Greek philosopher Aristotle boasted an impressive library and advised others on how to create their own. The first public library in Europe was established in Rome around 37 BC by Gaius Asinius Pollio, a contemporary of Julius Caesar and of the classical poets Virgil and Horace.

More than a millennium and a half later, in 1602, Sir Thomas Bodley founded the famous Bodleian Library at Oxford. In 1653, a prosperous Manchester textile merchant and banker, Humphrey Chetham, bequeathed to the city Chetham's Library, the oldest public library in the English-speaking world. The British Museum library, later to be housed in the dome-shaped Reading Room on the same Bloomsbury site, opened its doors to the public in 1753.

The eighteenth century saw the introduction of the circulating library, which operated on the basis of an annual subscription from readers. Like public libraries today, subscribers could borrow books for a fixed period of time, with fines imposed for late returns or any loss or damage. Fuelled by the growing popularity of the novel, circulating libraries sprang up around the country, becoming a key feature of the cultural scene. Subscription figures reached their peak in the mid-1800s with improvements in road, rail and the postal service speeding up distribution of the latest titles.

The spread of literacy and thirst for knowledge created a demand among the less well-off for free access to books. An 1850 Act of Parliament gave local boroughs the power to establish a public library within their community. The Lancashire town of Salford's Royal Museum and Public Library, opened in November 1850, was first off the blocks. The move spelled the end of the subscription library, though some would limp on until after the Second World War. For generations of dedicated readers, the local public library became the place to go.

BATTLE OF THE BOOKS

At the end of the seventeenth century, a fierce debate broke out among academics regarding the comparative merits of ancient and modern authors. Each side attracted vociferous support, though the Anglo-Irish satirist and poet Jonathan Swift (1667–1745) viewed the controversy with contempt. Swift, not known for suffering fools gladly, pitched in with a mock-heroic satire entitled *The Battle of the Books* (1704), which ridiculed the entire affair. In his sharply entertaining tale, books ancient and modern come to life and fight it out in London's St James's Library. The conflict is widened to include not just authors from the respective camps, but literary critics too. In an allegorical diversion to the main event, the bee is seen to represent the 'ancients' with the spider standing in for the 'moderns' (and the all-consuming critics). There is no definitive conclusion to the battle; Swift left it to the reader to decide which side comes out on top.

PICK UP A PENGUIN

In 1935, the publisher Allen Lane launched Britain's first mass market paperback imprint, beating the American Pocket Books Inc. to the draw by four years. He gave it the name Penguin (the avian nomenclature, in part inspired by the German publishing imprint Albatross) and followed it two years later with Pelican (specialist non-fiction) and, in 1940, Puffin (children's books). The first Penguin title was *Ariel*, a biography of the poet Percy Bysshe Shelley by the French writer André Maurois (1885–1967). Of the first ten Penguin books published (now collector's items) only two are well known today: Ernest Hemingway's *A Farewell to Arms* and *The Mysterious Affair at Styles* by Agatha Christie.

From the outset, Penguin's universal cover design was distinctively colour-coded to indicate the subject matter. Orange denoted general fiction; green was for crime; cerise for travel and adventure; dark blue for biography; and so on. After much soul-searching, Penguin made the move to pictorial covers in the 1960s, leaving some traditionalists unsure of what to pick up next.

THE COMING OF THE eBOOK

In 1949, a Spanish schoolteacher named Ángela Ruiz Robles, taking pity on students weighed down with text books, devised the world's first automated reader. Text and illustrations were contained on spools that were then loaded onto rotating spindles and viewed under a sheet of magnifying glass. The device, which the inventor christened the 'Mechanical Encyclopaedia', operated by means of compressed air. Her idea never advanced beyond the prototype stage, though it demonstrably worked and laid down a path for others to follow. Exactly half a century later eBooks became a publishing reality. In 1999, in America and for the first time, titles were published simultaneously in eBook and print formats. Readers could now choose whether to scroll down a page or simply turn it in the time-honoured tradition.

TEN BOOKS THAT CHANGED THE WORLD

The Qur'an (AD 609–632)
The founding text of Islam

King James Bible (1611)
Majestic English translation

First Folio (1623)
William Shakespeare
First major collection of the Bard's plays

Philosophiæ Naturalis Principia Mathematica (1687)
Sir Isaac Newton
A cornerstone of modern science

The Wealth of Nations (1776)
Adam Smith
Gospel of the free economy

The Communist Manifesto (1848)
Karl Marx/Friedrich Engels
Revolutionary handbook

On the Origin of Species (1859)
Charles Darwin
Breakthrough theory of evolution

The Interpretation of Dreams (1900)
Sigmund Freud
Exploration of the subconscious

The Second Sex (1949)
Simone de Beauvoir
Modern feminism begins here

Silent Spring (1962)
Rachel Carson
Kick-starting the environmental movement

NOVEL APPROACHES

'A good novel tells us the truth
about its hero; but a bad novel tells
us the truth about its author.'
G. K. CHESTERTON (1874-1936)

The seventeenth century saw the arrival of the modern novel, the English word 'novel' coming from the Italian *novella*, meaning a short tale. The literary form itself emerged from the pastoral and chivalric romances of the medieval period, which in turn evolved from earlier fictional narratives in prose or verse. *Don Quixote* by the Spanish writer Miguel de Cervantes is generally recognised as the first great modern novel. Published in two parts, in 1605 and 1615, the book mercilessly parodies the old chivalric tales with their improbable feats of derring-do, romances of knights in shining armour and damsels in distress. However, the scope and vision of the novel go beyond mere satire. In Don Quixote, the gentle madman who believes he is a knight errant, and Sancho Panza, the simple, portly (*panza* means 'belly') peasant who acts as his squire, Cervantes created two of the most enduring and beloved characters in world literature.

ROMAN REMAINS

One of the earliest examples of the novel form is the *Satyricon* by Petronius (Gaius Petronius Arbiter), published towards the end of the first century AD. Only a fragment of work, a mixture of prose and poetry, has survived. The satirical and episodic narrative, bawdy and richly entertaining, vividly portrays the vices and excesses of ancient Rome. It seems to have done the author (about whom we know practically nothing) little good. To avoid being executed by the emperor Nero, he took his own life *c.* AD 66.

The Golden Ass (also known as *Metamorphoses*) by Lucius Apuleius appeared several decades later (*c.* AD 155), and is the only Latin novel that has survived intact. The picaresque tale is about a young man (the narrator) whose insatiable curiosity results in him being turned into an ass, of the four-legged variety. There are 'sub-plots' of magic and love, one of which tells the story of Cupid and Psyche – later reproduced in paintings and in other literary forms.

NOVEL CASTAWAY

Daniel Defoe was born in London in 1660, five years before the devastating outbreak of bubonic plague in the city, about which he would later write a famous account – *A Journal of the Plague Year* (1722). Son of a London tallow-chandler, his surname was actually Foe; the gentrifying 'De' was added when the author was in his forties. After a career in trade, Defoe switched to writing, becoming a radical journalist and prolific pamphleteer. Impressively, he spoke six languages and could read a seventh. His dissenting views about the Church caused him to be fined, imprisoned and several times pilloried; on one occasion when he was in the stocks, his supporters formed a human shield to protect him from the usual missiles.

His first novel, *The Life and Adventures of Robinson Crusoe* (1719), was based on the real-life experiences of Alexander Selkirk, a castaway who had survived on a remote island for four years (though Defoe's hero is marooned for seven times as long). The book is written in the form of a personal memoir and can be viewed as the first English novel – not to mention the first survival manual. Despite the fact that he was already sixty when the book was published, Defoe went on to write several more novels, the best known of which is *Moll Flanders* (1722). The book's original title page almost says it all:

The
Fortunes & Misfortunes
of the Famous
Moll Flanders
&c.
who was Born in Newgate,
and during a Life of continu'd Variety
for Threescore Years, besides her Childhood,
was Twelve Year a Whore,
five time a Wife,
(whereof once to her own Brother)
Twelve Year a Thief,
Eight Year a Transported Felon
in Virginia,
at last grew rich,
liv'd Honest,
and died a Penitent.

WRITTEN FROM HER OWN MEMORANDUMS.

NOVEL TRENDS

As the novel developed, different ways of telling a story evolved, dictating the style as much as the content.

PICARESQUE NOVEL

The episodic adventures of the book's hero (whose name usually appears in the title), more often than not a likable rogue. Typically, there is a colourful cast of characters, plenty of amorous encounters and predictable confrontations with authority. All of which usually makes for a lengthy text. Early examples of this style of novel include Henry Fielding's *Tom Jones* (1749) and Tobias Smollett's *The Adventures of Peregrine Pickle* (1751). In the nineteenth century came Charles Dickens' *Pickwick Papers* (1837) and Mark Twain's *The Adventures of Huckleberry Finn* (1884), one of America's all-time great novels. Among recent picaresque works are the *Flashman* novels of George McDonald Fraser (1925–2008) and Jonas Jonasson's *The Hundred-Year-Old Man Who Climbed Out of the Window and Disappeared* (2009).

EPISTOLARY NOVEL

The English writer Samuel Richardson (1689–1761) was the early master of the epistolary novel, in which the story is told in the form of letters (or, nowadays, emails). The problem for the modern reader of Richardson's novels is their bulk, inflated by the author's moralising and tedious repetition. His most successful book, the tragic story of *Clarissa* (1747), runs close to a million words. A more entertaining example of the epistolary technique is *Les Liaisons Dangereuses* (*Dangerous Liaisons*) by Pierre Choderlos de Laclos (1741–1803), a tale of sexual shenanigans among aristos in pre-revolutionary France. Published in 1782, the book was later adapted for stage and screen by playwright

Christopher Hampton. Two red-letter novels of the genre in recent times are Lionel Shriver's *We Need to Talk About Kevin* (2003) and Aravind Adiga's *The White Tiger* (2008), winner of the Man Booker Prize.

GOTHIC NOVEL

Horace Walpole, all-round man of letters and the 4th Earl of Oxford (1717–97), was the author of the first English gothic novel: *The Castle of Otranto* (1764). The book laid down a blueprint for later works in the genre with its sinister location, evil central character, supernatural happenings and florid tone (fearing ridicule, Walpole initially hid behind a pseudonym, pretending the book was a translation from medieval Italian). The gothic novel has run and run. Ann Radcliffe (1764–1823), born the year Walpole's seminal book was published, wrote five influential novels of her own, the most popular of them *The Mysteries of Udolpho* (1790). Nineteenth-century blockbusters include Mary Shelley's *Frankenstein, or the Modern Prometheus* (1818), Robert Louis Stevenson's *The Strange Case of Dr Jekyll and Mr Hyde* (1886) and *Dracula* (1897) by Bram Stoker. Mervyn Peake's wonderfully weird *Gormenghast* trilogy (1946–59) took the gothic theme into greater realms of fantasy. While writers such as Stephen King, Anne Rice and Stephenie Meyer, with her vampire teens, have brought it up to date.

IT'S A FACT!

Lady Audley's Secret (1862) was one of the most sensational novels of the Victorian Age. Written by Mary Elizabeth Braddon (1835–1915), the plot involves bigamy, murder, arson and insanity – and that's just the titled lady herself. No wonder the Victorians lapped it up.

HISTORICAL NOVEL

The modern tradition of the historical novel – the factual past viewed through a fictional lens – began with Sir Walter Scott (1771–1832). Hugely popular and influential in his time (not to say prolific: he penned twenty-five bulky novels in the space of just eighteen years), his work is less well read today. His most famous book is *Ivanhoe* (1819), familiar to generations of filmgoers. The spectrum of the historical novel is vast, in terms of both subject matter and quality. At its pinnacle is Leo Tolstoy's *War and Peace* (1863–69), one of the greatest works of fiction ever. Among highly regarded modern examples of the genre are Robert Graves' *I, Claudius* (1934); Gore Vidal's series of novels on the history of America, which includes *Lincoln* (1984); Pat Barker's *Regeneration* trilogy (1991–95) set against the backdrop of the First World War; and Hilary Mantel's Tudor saga which began with *Wolf Hall* (2009).

IT'S A FACT!

Fewer than 4,000 copies of Herman Melville's novel *Moby Dick* (1851), generally recognised as one of the greatest American works of fiction, were sold in his lifetime. At the time of his death in 1891, the writer was so little known that the brief and belated obituary item in the *New York Times* referred to him as 'Hiram' Melville.

NOVEL OF MANNERS

This is supremely Jane Austen (1775–1817) territory. All six of her novels, starting with *Sense and Sensibility* (1811), brilliantly reflect the manners and mores of the middle-class provincial society in which she lived. Her characters are drawn accurately from real life and viewed with ironic detachment. The dialogue is masterly and the overall tone of the books much sharper than the sugary film adaptations. Elizabeth Gaskell (1810–65) was another writer, though not in the same league as Austen, who explored the contemporary social scene with novels such as *Cranford* (1853) and *North and South* (1855). New York society came under the wry scrutiny of the American author Edith Wharton in her 1905 novel *The House of Mirth*. Evelyn Waugh's *A Handful of Dust* (1934) and Nancy Mitford's *The Pursuit of Love* (1945) are later examples of the form; as is (if much less distinguished) the 2004 novel *Snobs* by Julian Fellowes, of *Downton Abbey* fame.

SATIRICAL NOVEL

Jonathan Swift's *Gulliver's Travels* (1726) is a stand-alone masterpiece. A satire on human nature and a lampooning of the contemporary craze for exotic travellers' tales, it was not conceived as a novel, though its imaginative storyline qualifies it as such. The French writer and philosopher Voltaire (1694–1778) came up with *Candide* (1759) which entertainingly satirises man's inhumanity to man (in 1958, the American writers Mason Hoffenberg and Terry Southern produced a raunchy version entitled *Candy*, switching the sex of the eponymous central character). Among the best modern satirical novels are Evelyn Waugh's *Decline and Fall* (1928); Joseph Heller's anti-war black comedy *Catch-22* (1961); Kurt Vonnegut's absurdist take on the firebombing of Dresden, *Slaughterhouse Five* (1969); Tom Sharpe's send-up of university life, *Porterhouse Blue* (1974); and *The Sellout* (2015) by American novelist Paul Beatty, winner of the 2016 Man Booker Prize.

MAGIC REALISM NOVEL

This is a form of the novel that has become popular in recent years, with fantastic or mythical elements incorporated into an otherwise realistic narrative. *The Master and Margarita* by the Russian writer Mikhail Bulgakov (1891–1940) is an exhilarating example of the style. Bulgakov, a victim of Soviet censorship, finished the novel just before his death but it was to be another twenty-five years before the book was published. Salman Rushdie (1947–) is among those who have contributed to the genre, notably with his breakthrough novel *Midnight's Children* (1981). Magic realism is most associated with Latin American fiction, and in particular with Gabriel García Márquez (1927–2014) and Isabel Allende (1942–). The Colombian Márquez, who won the Nobel Prize in Literature in 1982, employed the technique in many of his works, starting with the acclaimed *One Hundred Years of Solitude* (1967). Isabel Allende, Chilean though born in Peru, joined the club with her bestselling debut novel, *The House of the Spirits* (1982).

KEEPING IT SHORT

For many writers, the short story has been a prelude to longer works of fiction. Others have made it their chosen métier. Here are ten of its finest exponents.

Author	Sample story
Guy de Maupassant (1850–93)	'The Necklace'
Anton Chekhov (1860–1904)	'The Lady with the Dog'
O. Henry (1862–1910)	'The Gift of the Magi'
Katherine Mansfield (1888–1923)	'The Garden Party'
Ernest Hemingway (1899–1961)	'The Killers'

W. Somerset Maugham (1874–1965)	'Rain'
John Cheever (1912–82)	'The Swimmer'
Raymond Carver (1938–88)	'Vitamins'
Roald Dahl (1916–90)	'Lamb to the Slaughter'
Alice Munro (1931–)	'The Bear Came over the Mountain'

GRAND MASTERS

The novel came into its own in the nineteenth century at the hands of some of the greatest masters of the form. At times, masterpieces were almost tripping over each other.

The 1830s in France saw the publication of Stendhal's (real name Marie-Henri Beyle) two influential historical novels, *The Red and the Black* (1830) and *The Charterhouse of Parma* (1839); *The Hunchback of Notre Dame* (1831) by Victor Hugo; and two of Honoré de Balzac's finest works, *Eugénie Grandet* (1833) and *Le Père Goriot* (*Old Goriot*, 1835).

The year 1847 was an *annus mirabilis* for the three tragic Brontë sisters, with the publication of Charlotte's *Jane Eyre*, Emily's *Wuthering Heights* and Anne's *Agnes Grey*. A year later, William Makepeace Thackeray's *Vanity Fair* hit the bookshops, launching the career of one of literature's great femmes fatales, Becky Sharp.

Two iconic but contrasting American novels came out in successive years. *The Scarlet Letter* (1850) by Nathaniel Hawthorne is a study of adultery and guilt in seventeenth-century New England. Herman Melville's brooding work *Moby Dick* (1851) tells of Captain Ahab's obsessive pursuit of the eponymous white whale that in a previous encounter had chewed off his leg.

Three Russian masterpieces coincided in the 1860s, Ivan Turgenev's *Fathers and Sons* (1862) and Fyodor Dostoevsky's *Crime and Punishment* (1866) lining up alongside Leo Tolstoy's *War and Peace* (1863–69). Tolstoy and Dostoevsky never met but, unusually for literary heavyweights sharing the ring, they had a high regard for each other's work.

Other landmark novels of the century include Gustave Flaubert's *Madame Bovary* (1857) and George Eliot's *Middlemarch* (1872), presenting two very different views of provincial life. Émile Zola's *Germinal* (1885) followed and it depicts with brutal realism the plight of the French coal-mining community – one of a series of twenty scrupulously detailed (and, for the time, shockingly explicit) social novels spanning generations of the Rougon-Macquart family.

Then there was Charles Dickens.

SERIAL RIGHTS

Charles Dickens (1812–70) is considered by many to be Britain's greatest novelist. Each of his fifteen novels first appeared in serial form, starting with *Pickwick Papers* in 1836. Serialisation of his final novel, *The Mystery of Edwin Drood*, was interrupted by the author's death. The instalments appeared weekly or monthly, many of them in magazines founded by Dickens himself. Writing them in serial form explains the unwieldy structure of many of the plots and the multiplicity of characters, prompting George Orwell's famous observation of Dickens' novels: 'rotten architecture, wonderful gargoyles' (i.e. characters).

Victorian readers were hooked on the unfolding stories (fortunately for Dickens, serialisation didn't adversely affect sales of the novels in book form), clamouring for each new episode. It is said that when copies of the final part of *The Old Curiosity Shop* (1841) arrived by ship in New York, the crowd gathered on the quayside shouted to the crew, 'Is Little Nell dead?' Some fans were ahead of the game. The American writer Edgar Allan Poe came up with a solution to the murder in *Barnaby Rudge* (1841) while the novel was still being serialised in a magazine. He published his version of events in the *Saturday Evening Post*, before the revealing episode had reached America. Not only did he correctly solve the crime but, as Dickens later acknowledged, he had worked it out even before the author himself.

IT'S A FACT!

The Prague-born German writer Franz Kafka (1883–1924) left instructions that on his death from tuberculosis, all his unpublished manuscripts were to be burned. His editor ignored the request and Kafka's only three novels – *The Trial* (1924), *The Castle* (1926) and *Amerika* (1927) – survived to tell the tale.

INAUSPICIOUS MEETING

Two men who turned the novel on its head met for the one and only time on 19 May 1922. Marcel Proust (1871–1922) was midway through the publication of his monumental novel *À la Recherche du Temps Perdu* (originally published in English as *Remembrance of Things Past*), which was drip fed to the French public in seven volumes between 1913 and 1927, the last three published posthumously. The semi-autobiographical novel, a convoluted exercise in memory set amongst the French upper class, had taken the cultural scene by storm.

James Joyce's (1882–1941) *Ulysses*, with its stream-of-consciousness style, recorded the events of a single day in the Dublin lives of its three central characters. The book, which had just been published in Paris, would be banned in the UK and USA for more than a decade.

The meeting took place at a private dinner party at the Hôtel Majestic in Paris. The composer Igor Stravinsky and director of the Russian Ballet Sergei Diaghilev were also in attendance. Joyce arrived late, shabbily dressed and a little drunk. The hypochondriac Proust, making a rare excursion from his cork-lined germ-free room where he normally worked at night and slept by day, was expensively swaddled in a fur coat. There are differing accounts of their brief encounter, though all agree that few words were exchanged and there was no rapport between the two great writers. Neither had read the other's work.

IT'S A FACT!

An interviewer once tactlessly said to Joseph Heller (1923–99) that the author had never written anything else as good as his 1961 novel *Catch-22*. To which Heller snappily retorted, 'Who has?'

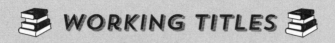

WORKING TITLES

Famous novels that were nearly called something else.

Pride and Prejudice (1813) Jane Austen	*First Impressions*
War and Peace (1863–9) Leo Tolstoy	*All's Well That Ends Well*
Treasure Island (1883) Robert Louis Stevenson	*The Sea-Cook*
The Great Gatsby (1925) F. Scott Fitzgerald	*Incident at West Egg*
Lady Chatterley's Lover (1928) D. H. Lawrence	*Tenderness*
Gone with the Wind (1936) Margaret Mitchell	*Baa! Baa! Black Sheep*
Nineteen Eighty-Four (1949) George Orwell	*The Last Man in Europe*
Catch-22 (1961) Joseph Heller	*Catch-18*
Portnoy's Complaint (1969) Philip Roth	*A Jewish Patient Begins His Analysis*
Jaws (1974) Peter Benchley	*A Silence in the Water*

BAN THE BOOK

'*God forbid that any book should be banned.*
The practice is as indefensible as infanticide.'
REBECCA WEST (1892–1983)

From the moment books came into being, people found reasons to ban them. The Catholic Church's *Index Librorum Prohibitorum (List of Prohibited Books)* lasted from 1559 to 1966 and at one time cited more than 5,000 forbidden works. Many famous novelists were proscribed, from Laurence Sterne in 1819 to the two Alexandre Dumas in 1863, father and son entering the list together. Also banned were the philosophical works of Thomas Hobbes in 1649 and Jean-Jacques Rousseau in 1762, and Edward Gibbons' *The Decline and Fall of the Roman Empire* (1783). The French novelist and philosopher Jean-Paul Sartre was outlawed in 1948, his partner Simone de Beauvoir joining him on the list eight years later. Books were banned because they were deemed heretical, anti-clerical, licentious or obscene – which covered a lot of ground.

In the 1930s, the Nazis made bonfires out of books that didn't fit their warped philosophy. International reputations counted for nothing. Persecuted Austrian and German authors included Sigmund Freud and Albert Einstein, the playwright Bertolt Brecht and the novelist Thomas Mann. Among foreign writers whose works were committed to the flames were Victor Hugo, Ernest Hemingway, Jack London, D. H. Lawrence, Joseph Conrad, Leo Tolstoy, James Joyce and Marcel Proust.

In the Soviet Union (as in the time of the tsars) there was heavy censorship and many works were suppressed altogether. Some Russian authors were sent to labour camps, a fate experienced by the Nobel Prize winner Alexander Solzhenitsyn (1918–2008). Others, like the greatly admired short story writer Isaac Babel (1894–1940), were executed in Stalin's purges.

IT'S A FACT!

Maurice Sendak's 1970 children's picture-book classic *In the Night Kitchen* was withdrawn from many school and public libraries in America because of the full frontal nudity of the young central character, Mickey.

RADICAL IDEAS

Thomas Paine (1737–1809) was born in Norfolk, the son of a Quaker corset-maker. He travelled to America in 1774 and became an influential supporter of American independence, his views expressed in a widely read pamphlet, *Common Sense* (1776). Paine, who advocated revolt rather than reform, returned to England in 1787. There he wrote *The Rights of Man* (1791), a political work that defended the French Revolution, which had started a couple of years before. The book, published in two parts, made dangerous waves; Prime Minister William Pitt commented: 'Tom Paine is quite in the right... but if I were to encourage his opinion we should have a bloody revolution.'

Paine was charged with sedition and, tipped off by the artist and poet William Blake, fled to France before he could be arrested. At first he was welcomed across the Channel as a revolutionary hero, but his opposition to the bloody extremes of the 'Reign of Terror' nearly resulted in his being guillotined himself. Back in the USA, Paine turned his radical sights on religion in *The Age of Reason* (1796). The book was reviled by his former allies, who denounced him as an atheist. It was a revolutionary step too far.

SHOCKING BEHAVIOUR

One of the most acclaimed and influential novels of the twentieth century, *The Catcher in the Rye* (1951) by J. D. Salinger (1919–2010), was banned by many American schools and libraries in the years following its publication. Parent groups expressed concern about the effects of the book on impressionable teenagers. Salinger's iconic coming-of-age story relates the adventures of the infectiously rebellious 16-year-old Holden Caulfield, on route to New York after having been expelled from his school. The book was banned for its vulgar language, sexual references, depiction of alcohol abuse (mainly by Holden himself) and for its general anti-social stance, though it is now required reading on many school and university syllabuses. It didn't help the book's reputation that John Lennon's killer, Mark Chapman, was an obsessive fan of the work.

FORBIDDEN FRUITS

Sir Arthur Conan Doyle's *The Adventures of Sherlock Holmes* was banned in Russia in 1929 because of the author's interest in occultism and spiritualism, though neither features in the collected stories. *Alice's Adventures in Wonderland*, by Lewis Carroll, suffered a similar fate in the Hunan province of China in 1931, though for a different reason: the Chinese authorities objected to animals being put on a par with humans and speaking their language.

Ernest Hemingway's 1929 novel *A Farewell to Arms* was initially banned in Italy because of its humiliatingly accurate account of the Italian retreat (against Austro-Hungarian forces) at the Battle of Caporetto in 1917. The children's classic *Black Beauty* (1877), by Anna Sewell, fell foul of South Africa's apartheid regime due to the juxtaposition of 'black' and 'beauty' in the title. Dan Brown's international blockbuster *The Da Vinci Code* (2003) was outlawed in Lebanon on the grounds that it was offensive to Christians, with French, Arabic and English editions all removed from the shelves.

Following the publication of James Joyce's *Ulysses* in Paris in 1922 (on his fortieth birthday), customs authorities in England, the USA and his native Ireland burned copies of the book. A celebrated court judgement in America lifted the ban in 1934 and the first UK edition was published two years later. Another literary masterpiece to get off to a shaky start was Vladimir Nabokov's *Lolita* (1956) about a middle-aged professor's obsession with a precocious 12-year-old nymphet. The book was banned briefly in France, England, Belgium and Argentina, before becoming established as a modern classic.

UNINFORMED DECISION

Bury My Heart at Wounded Knee (1970) by the historian Dee Brown (1908–2002) is an account of the United States' westward expansion during the latter half of the nineteenth century and its dire consequences for Native Americans. The book, with its shocking revelations about aspects of American government policy at the time, was a critical and commercial success. However, in 1974, a school administrator in Wild Rose, Wisconsin, banned the book – without reading it – on the grounds that it was 'slanted'. When asked to defend his decision, the education official said: 'If there's a possibility that something might be controversial, then why not ban it?'

LADY CHATTERLEY ON TRIAL

D. H. Lawrence's controversial novel, *Lady Chatterley's Lover*, was first published privately in Italy in 1928. The story of an aristocratic wife who has an affair with her (physically and emotionally) crippled husband's gamekeeper is told in language that is remarkably ripe and explicit for its time, as are the many sexual bouts in the book. Lawrence (1885–1930) had form, having written two previous novels that had attracted censorship problems, *The Rainbow* (1915) and *Women in Love* (1920). The book eventually came out in the UK in a bowdlerised version – minus all its four-letter words – and remained that way until 1960, when Penguin Books published an unexpurgated edition of the novel.

The publishers were deemed to be in breach of the Obscene Publications Act and were taken to court. The Crown versus Penguin Books began on 21 October 1960. For the six days of the trial the literary glitterati queued up to speak on behalf of Lawrence (long since dead) and his novel. It didn't help the Crown's case when the prosecuting counsel, completely out of touch with the changing social mores of the time, asked one of the witnesses: 'Is it a book that you would even wish your wife or your servants to read?' The jury took just three hours to acquit the defendants, and the cash registers started to ring.

IT'S A FACT!

Grace Metalious (1925–64), author of the lusty bestseller *Peyton Place* (1956), once described herself as a 'lousy writer' but went on to say that a 'helluva lot of people have got lousy taste'.

SATANIC CLAIMS

Salman Rushdie's novel *The Satanic Verses* prompted a fierce reaction from many Muslims when published in 1988. The author was accused of blasphemy and of taking the prophet Muhammad's name in vain. In a startling turn of events, Iran's religious leader, the Ayatollah Khomeini, issued a fatwa instructing Muslims to assassinate Rushdie. The threatened writer went into hiding with round-the-clock protection from Special Branch. He issued a public apology, which was rejected by the Ayatollah. There were demonstrations in Britain and elsewhere in the world; many countries banned the book. Several London bookshops were bombed, and in the city of Bradford, copies of the novel were publicly burned.

In the first year of the fatwa, Rushdie and his wife moved home more than fifty times. Their marriage broke up under the strain. Ignited by the controversy, sales of the book soared on both sides of the Atlantic. *The Satanic Verses* won the 1988 Whitbread Novel of the Year award, with its prize of £20,000. Although the threat has receded, the fatwa on Rushdie's life has not been withdrawn. His account of those turbulent days was published in 2012, in the form of a memoir written in the third person. The book is titled *Joseph Anton* – a nod to Joseph Conrad and Anton Chekhov, and the pseudonym used by Rushdie when in hiding.

 TO COIN A WORD

Many words in everyday use were coined by writers, though in some cases the original meaning has shifted somewhat. The word 'pandemonium', for example, first appeared in John Milton's epic poem *Paradise Lost* (1667) as the name of Satan's city, the place where all the demons hang out.

'Yahoos' was the name Jonathan Swift gave to a race of brutish human-like creatures in his satirical work *Gulliver's Travels* (1726), before the term was downgraded to describe people of a generally loutish disposition. Sir Thomas More, later decapitated by Henry VIII, gave birth to *Utopia* (1516), the eponymous fictional island with its near-perfect society that is the subject of his philosophical tome. We have Dr Seuss to thank for 'nerd', one of the imaginary animals in his children's story *If I Ran the Zoo* (1950), though the modern definition of the word arrived much later.

Lewis Carroll came up with 'chortle' (a hybrid of chuckle and snort) in *Through the Looking-Glass*

(1871). The word 'mentor' stems from Mentor, teacher and trusted adviser to Odysseus's son Telemachus in Homer's *Odyssey*. In François Rabelais' monumental medieval fantasy *Gargantua and Pantagruel* (*c.*1532–64), the giant hero Gargantua is born via his mother's left ear and emerges from the 'womb' sporting a yard-long erection, giving rise to the word 'gargantuan'.

'Freelance' first popped up in Sir Walter Scott's novel *Ivanhoe* (1819), referring to mercenaries offering to fight for a fee. The pejorative term 'banana republic' made its debut in O. Henry's *Cabbages and Kings* (1904), a collection of linked short stories set in Central America. The word 'mole', to describe someone who works for an organisation or government department and secretly hands on sensitive information to an enemy or rival, passed into common usage courtesy of John le Carré's spy novel *Tinker, Tailor, Soldier, Spy* (1974).

However, few modern writers have added more to the language than George Orwell, whose dystopian novel *Nineteen Eighty-Four* (finished in 1948 and published a year later) produced 'newspeak', 'doublethink', 'thoughtcrime' and the titles of two future television programmes, *Big Brother* and *Room 101*. All of which might be said to be very 'Orwellian'.

WRITERS' FEUDS

'*Writers seldom wish other writers well.*'
SAUL BELLOW (1915-2005)

Writers are a competitive bunch. They jealously monitor the success of their rivals and darkly catalogue their own all-too-public failures. Sensitive to any criticism or slur, real or imagined, they respond with the weapons closest to hand: words. Over the years this has sparked some lively literary feuds.

LORD BYRON v JOHN KEATS

Socially they were poles apart. George Gordon Byron, 6th Baron Byron of Rochdale (1788–1824), was educated at Harrow and Cambridge before taking his seat in the House of Lords. The publication, in 1812, of Byron's long narrative poem *Childe Harold's Pilgrimage* had catapulted the poet to fame. His flamboyant lifestyle added to his public celebrity and, in the words of Lady Caroline Lamb, with whom he had a well-documented affair, Byron was 'mad, bad, and dangerous to know'. John Keats (1795–1821) was the London-born son of a livery-stable keeper, leaving school at the age of fifteen to become apprenticed to an apothecary. A medical student at a London hospital, he struggled to make ends meet and to get his poetry published.

Byron, among others, snobbishly dismissed Keats as a mere 'Cockney poet'. In a letter to his own publisher John Murray, he more graphically referred to 'Johnny Keats' piss-a-bed poetry', adding, 'there is no bearing the drivelling idiotism of the Mankin' ('little man'). Meanwhile, as far as Keats was concerned, Byron's work lacked originality and was overrated by his adoring readers. His success, he claimed, was all down to the poet's aristocratic pedigree and glamorous image. He once bitterly observed to a friend: 'You see what it is to be six foot tall and a lord!'

IT'S A FACT!

Few 'words' between eminent writers have been more vitriolic than those exchanged by American man of letters Ralph Waldo Emerson (1803–82) and English poet Algernon Charles Swinburne (1837–1909). The latter unpoetically described Emerson as 'a gap-toothed and hoary-headed ape'. While to the American, Swinburne was 'a perfect leper, and a mere sodomite'.

MARK TWAIN v BRET HARTE

They started as friends and collaborators. Born in Hannibal, Missouri, Mark Twain (1835–1910) gravitated to San Francisco where he met Bret Harte, a poet and writer of short stories and editor of a journal called *The Overland Monthly*. The more experienced Harte (1836–1902), whose humorous tales about Californian gold miners were very popular, helped smooth the rough edges of Twain's apprentice literary style. The two men transferred to the East Coast and decided to co-write a play, which they titled *Ah Sin* (1877). It proved to be a disastrous collaboration.

The root of the problem was not artistic but financial. Harte asked Twain for a loan, which the latter refused. Instead, he proposed paying Harte a weekly salary of $25 to work on a second play. This time it was Harte, insulted by the offer, who refused. The two men fell out, avoiding each other's company even on the opening night of their play. That same year, Harte was considered for a diplomatic post overseas. Twain took the extraordinary step of writing to the American president, James Garfield, in an effort to block the appointment. To an intermediary he wrote: 'Harte is a liar, a thief, a swindler, a snob, a sot, a sponge, a coward, a Jeremy Diddler, he is brim full of treachery.' Harte did get a job as a United States consul, but no thanks to his former partner. Even after Harte's death in 1902, Mark Twain pursued the vendetta. In a volume of autobiography, he recalled: 'In the early days I liked Bret Harte . . . but by and by I got over it.'

LITERARY PUNCH-UP

In 1997, an unseemly public spat broke out between two of Britain's most distinguished writers, Salman Rushdie and John le Carré. The origin of the row dated back some eight years to *The Satanic Verses* controversy, when le Carré had accused Rushdie of potentially risking people's lives by insisting that his publishers go ahead with the paperback edition of the book. Now Rushdie criticised le Carré for overreacting to a lone reviewer's accusation of anti-Semitism in the latter's latest book *The Tailor of Panama* (1996). The two writers went at each other hammer and tongs in a series of angry exchanges in *The Guardian*. The quarrel eventually ran its course but it would be another fifteen years before there was a reconciliation between them.

HENRY JAMES v H. G. WELLS

Herbert George Wells (1866–1946) burst onto the British publishing scene with his science-fiction novel *The Time Machine* (1895), followed in the space of three years by *The Island of Doctor Moreau* (1896), *The Invisible Man* (1897) and *The War of the Worlds* (1898) – all destined to become classics of the genre. An early admirer of his talent was the American-born novelist and short story writer Henry James (1843–1916), who had made England his home since the 1870s. James, the pre-eminent American writer of his time, dubbed 'The Master', heaped praise on the young Wells: 'You are, for me... the most interesting "literary man" of your generation – in fact, the only interesting one.'

It wasn't to last. The two men didn't agree on the nature of literature, or on its role in society. For James, its importance was simply as an art form, the creative composition an end in its own right. For Wells, a trained biologist and political reformist, literature was essentially a tool for expressing ideas. Their differences, exchanged in a series of letters, were irreconcilable. In 1915, a year before the older man's death, Wells published a satirical novel entitled *Boon*, in which he caricatured James and parodied his verbose style of writing, likening it to a hippopotamus trying to pick up a pea in the corner of its den. A wounded but ever-courteous Henry James mildly rebuked the author for the 'bad manners of *Boon*', which finally drew a line under their relationship.

NORMAN MAILER v GORE VIDAL

Two of the brightest stars of America's post-war literary scene, Norman Mailer and Gore Vidal were destined to collide. Mailer (1923–2007) was born in New Jersey to middle-class Jewish parents. A precocious student at Harvard University at the age of sixteen, he had his first short story published two years later. Vidal (1925–2012) was a child of the Washington political establishment. His grandfather was a famous senator, his father a high-flyer in the burgeoning aviation business. Both writers produced first novels based on their wartime experiences, with Mailer's *The Naked and the Dead* (1948) infinitely the more successful. Both unsuccessfully ran for political office, Mailer for Mayor of New York, Vidal for the US Senate. Mailer won two Pulitzer Prizes (one fiction, one non-fiction); Vidal was a brilliant essayist and Broadway playwright. Both men had egos to match their achievements.

They knew each other well, but the relationship was always edgy. In 1971, in reviewing Mailer's book about the feminist movement, *The Prisoner of Sex*, Vidal provocatively compared the author to the killer Charles Manson. When the two writers later met on *The Dick Cavett Show*, Mailer angrily brought up the subject (in the hospitality room earlier, he had thrown a punch at Vidal). A visibly nervous Cavett managed to defuse the situation, though it made for riveting television. Six years later, at a New York gathering in honour of Princess Margaret, the pugnacious Mailer threw a drink in Vidal's face then punched him in the mouth. The bloodied Vidal's response was typically verbal: 'Norman, once again words have failed you.' In 1984, Mailer called a truce – an uneasy peace which lasted the rest of their lives.

The novelist and literary critic Cyril Connolly (1903–74) once spitefully described fellow writer Vita Sackville-West (1892–1962) as looking 'like Lady Chatterley above the waist, and the gamekeeper below.'

GABRIEL GARCÍA MÁRQUEZ v MARIO VARGAS LLOSA

During the 1960s, Latin America's two literary giants had been friends and one-time roommates. The Colombian Márquez (1927–2014) achieved international fame with his 1967 novel *One Hundred Years of Solitude*. Vargas Llosa, nine years his junior and from neighbouring Peru, followed suit with *Conversation in the Cathedral* (1969). In the way of modern itinerant writers, they flitted from country to country, crossing paths from time to time. In 1976, they bumped into each other in Mexico City.

It was Valentine's Day and the two amigos had been attending the premiere of a documentary about the survivors of a plane crash in the Andes. As the story goes, Márquez warmly greeted his friend outside the cinema, arms outstretched: 'Mario!' Llosa's response was to punch Márquez in the eye, shouting: 'How dare you come and greet me after what you did to Patricia [Llosa's second wife] in Barcelona!' Patricia, it seems, had sought consolation from 'Gabo' after Llosa had temporarily left home in romantic pursuit of someone else. The matter appeared to hinge on just what form the consolation had taken. Whatever the truth, Márquez displayed a shining black eye to the press the following day and the two men didn't speak to each other for thirty-one years. A reconciliation of sorts took place in 2007.

When Llosa was awarded the Nobel Prize in 2010 (Márquez had picked up his in 1982), his erstwhile friend was among the first to congratulate him.

PAUL THEROUX v V. S. NAIPAUL

The American writer Paul Theroux was teaching at the university in Kampala, Uganda, when he first met V. S. Naipaul. It was 1966 and the Trinidadian-born novelist was a visiting scholar. The two men became friends and when Theroux moved to the UK a few years later, Naipaul acted as his guide and mentor. Theroux (father of Louis Theroux, the documentary filmmaker) achieved international fame with his bestselling travel book *The Great Railway Bazaar* (1975). Naipaul's own reputation had continued to grow, his early comic novels giving way to a much bleaker view of the world (one that would earn him the Nobel Prize in 2001). However, when the American wrote critically of Naipaul's work, the relationship between the two men cooled.

Things came to a head when Theroux spotted copies of his books, affectionately inscribed to Naipaul and his first wife Pat, on sale in a rare books catalogue. When he confronted Naipaul about the matter, the latter brushed him aside, saying: 'Take it on the chin and move on.' Their spat became public in 1998 when Theroux published *Sir Vidia's Shadow: A Friendship Across Five Continents*, a memoir which portrayed Naipaul in an unattractive light. The feud lasted fifteen years. Then, in 2011, fellow author Ian McEwan helped broker a reconciliation at the Hay Literary Festival. The two men shook hands, paving the way for a happy ending.

No one can say writers don't move with the times, even when it comes to abuse. In 2012, Bret Easton Ellis, author of *American Psycho* (1991), took to Twitter to attack fellow novelist David Foster Wallace, four years after the latter had committed suicide. He described the acclaimed author of the 1996 novel *Infinite Jest* as tedious, overrated, tortuous, pretentious and a fraud.

A. S. BYATT v MARGARET DRABBLE

The sibling rivalry began in childhood. Antonia Susan Drabble was born in Sheffield in 1936, her sister Margaret three years later. Brought up in a competitive family environment, both girls were groomed to be high academic achievers by their teacher mother, who was determined they should win a place at Newnham College, Cambridge, to read English as she had done. Her ambition was fulfilled, with Margaret, following her sister to university, coming away with a superior degree. Margaret, who originally intended a career on the stage, was also the first to have a novel published (*A Summer Bird Cage*, 1963), which didn't thrill Antonia who was still working on *her* first book. Three years later, A. S. Byatt (her married name), now up and running as a novelist, published *The Game* – a story of a painful sibling rivalry, which wasn't hard to decode. She sent her sister a copy with an apology attached. Drabble described the book as 'mean-spirited'.

Since then the two women have frostily kept their distance. Drabble claims to have read only one of Byatt's subsequent novels, *Possession*, which won the 1990 Booker Prize. Their literary careers (not restricted to fiction) have run neck and neck, and between them they have picked up around twenty major awards.

Both have been made a Dame for their services to literature. Services to each other is something else.

TOM WOLFE v JOHN IRVING, NORMAN MAILER AND JOHN UPDIKE

Tom Wolfe (1931–) leapt to fame in the late 1960s with a gaudy new style of journalism that brilliantly tapped into America's liberated social scene. His linguistic pyrotechnics were reflected in the titles of books such as *The Kandy-Kolored Tangerine-Flake Streamline Baby* (1965) and *The Electric Kool-Aid Acid Test* (1968). A skilled self-publicist, Wolfe made himself instantly recognisable with his trademark white suit, hat and shoes. In 1987, he turned to fiction with *The Bonfire of the Vanities*, a critical and commercial success. His second novel, *A Man in Full* (1998), took him a decade to write.

Two of America's most eminent men of letters, Norman Mailer and John Updike, panned the new novel. Updike dismissed it as 'entertainment, not literature, even literature in a modest, aspirant form'. Mailer compared reading the voluminous text to making love to a 300-lb woman: 'Once she gets on top, it's over. Fall in love, or be asphyxiated.' The wounded Wolfe responded by referring to the pair as 'two old piles of bones'. At which point fellow novelist John Irving (*The World According to Garp* and *The Cider House Rules*) weighed in. Of Wolfe's fiction, he said: 'It's like reading a bad newspaper or a bad piece in a magazine. It makes you wince.' He then went on to say that on any page of a Wolfe novel he could 'read a sentence that would make me gag'. The man in the white suit retaliated by comparing his distinguished critics to the Three Stooges – Larry, Curly and Moe. 'It must gall them a bit that everyone, even them, is talking about me.'

SHAFTING THE OPPOSITION

'With the single exception of Homer, there is no eminent writer, not even Sir Walter Scott, whom I can despise so entirely as I despise Shakespeare when I measure my mind against his... It would positively be a relief to me to dig Shakespeare up and throw stones at him.'
George Bernard Shaw (1856–1950)

'There are two ways of disliking poetry; one way is to dislike it, the other is to read Pope.'
Oscar Wilde (1854–1900) on Alexander Pope (1688–1744)

'He was dull in company, dull in his closet, dull everywhere. He was dull in a new way, and that made many people think him GREAT. He was a mechanical poet.'
Samuel Johnson (1709–84) on Thomas Gray (1716–71)

'Gibbon is an ugly, affected, disgusting fellow, and poisons our literary club for me. I class him among infidel wasps and venomous insects.'
James Boswell (1740–95) on Edward Gibbon (1737–94)

'He was a liar and a cheat; he paid no regard to truth, nor to any kind of moral obligation.'
Robert Southey (1774–1843) on Percy Bysshe Shelley (1792–1822)

'His manners are to 99 in 100 singularly repulsive.'
Samuel Taylor Coleridge (1772–1834) on William Hazlitt (1778–1830)

'Wordsworth has left a bad impression wherever he visited in town by his egotism, vanity, and bigotry.'
John Keats (1795–1821) on William Wordsworth (1770–1850)

'You know I can't stand Shakespeare's plays, but yours are even worse.'
Leo Tolstoy (1828–1910) to Anton Chekhov (1860–1904)

'Very poor stuff. I think he was mentally defective.'
Evelyn Waugh (1903–66) on Marcel Proust (1871–1922)

'[H. G.] Wells was a cad who didn't pretend to be anything but a cad. [Arnold] Bennett was a cad pretending to be a gentleman. [George Bernard] Shaw was a gentleman pretending to be a cad.'
Hilaire Belloc (1870–1953)

'Her mind is a very thin soil, laid an inch or two upon very barren rock.'
Virginia Woolf (1882–1941) on Katherine Mansfield (1888–1923)

'That old lady is a crashing bore.'
Dorothy Parker (1893–1967) about W. Somerset Maugham (1874–1965)

'He was a detestable man. Men pressed money on him, and women their bodies. Dylan took both with

equal contempt. His great pleasure was to humiliate people.'
A. J. P. Taylor (1906–90) on Dylan Thomas (1914–53)

'I read him for the first time in the early forties, something about bells, balls and bulls, and loathed it.'
Vladimir Nabokov (1899–1977) on Ernest Hemingway (1899–1961)

'Kerouac lacks discipline, intelligence, honesty and a sense of the novel. His rhythms are erratic, his sense of character is nil, and he is as pretentious as a rich whore, as sentimental as a lollipop.'
Norman Mailer (1923–2007) on Jack Kerouac (1922–69)

'A poet who never wrote an original line.'
Robert Graves (1895–1985) on W. H. Auden (1907–73)

'Every word she writes is a lie, including "and" and "the".'
Mary McCarthy (1912–89) on Lillian Hellman (1905–84)

'I don't think William Burroughs [1914–97] has an ounce of talent.'
Truman Capote (1924–84)

'I think you judge Truman too charitably when you call him a child; he is more like a sweetly vicious old lady.'
Tennessee Williams (1911–83) on Truman Capote (1924–84)

WRITERS AT WORK

'A blank piece of paper
is God's way of telling us how
hard it is to be God.'
SIDNEY SHELDON (1917–2007)

The principal tool of the trade for most modern writers is the computer, a depository for the painstakingly crafted words as well as a useful research engine. Some authors, though, prefer a less high-tech approach.

The American novelist and short story writer Joyce Carol Oates composes in longhand, as does British author John le Carré. Neil Gaiman, whose fantasy fiction includes *American Gods* (2001) and the children's novel *The Graveyard Book* (2008), is another who writes by hand, though he resorts to a computer for screenplays. J. K. Rowling wrote the earlier drafts of *Harry Potter and the Philosopher's Stone* (1997) in longhand, before graduating to a vintage typewriter. Others who find creative comfort in a typewriter are the authors Julian Barnes and Will Self, the playwright Alan Bennett and the prolific American novelist Danielle Steel, all of whose international blockbusters have been written on the same 1946 manual machine, for which she forked out the princely sum of $20, second-hand.

Leo Tolstoy rewrote his monumental novel *War and Peace* (1863–69) at least seven times. Each time his wife Sofia, the only person who could read his handwriting, had to copy out the text.

ON THE JOB

Today's professional writer is likely to follow a regular routine, many preferring to do their creative work during the morning shift, leaving the afternoon for revisions or research (or even recreation), or for catching up on correspondence. Some of their predecessors had a more idiosyncratic approach to their craft. Two of the world's greatest novelists, Fyodor Dostoevsky and Marcel Proust, both wrote through the night. Gustave Flaubert, author of the French classic *Madame Bovary* (1857), routinely put pen to paper from midday to 4 a.m., smoking some fifteen pipefuls of tobacco along the way. The Belgian-born writer Georges Simenon (1903–89), who wrote close to 500 novels in all, half of them published under various pseudonyms when he was learning his craft, typically knocked off a new work in ten or eleven days at the most, locking himself in his study for the duration and having meals left outside the door. Before embarking on this rigorous schedule, in later years, he took the precaution of having a medical check-up.

Writers who went about their task standing up, using a lectern or some suitably elevated worktop, include Lewis Carroll, Virginia Woolf, the American novelist Thomas Wolfe (not to be confused with his later namesake Tom Wolfe), Vladimir Nabokov and Ernest Hemingway. Philip Roth, author of *Portnoy's Complaint* (1969) and *The Human Stain* (2000), chose to write at a lectern to spare a troublesome back.

WRITER'S BLOCK

The ailment most feared by authors is 'writer's block': a sudden, irrational inability to put words on paper. Many famous writers from Leo Tolstoy to Philip Larkin have suffered from it; a few terminally. The American crime writer Dashiell Hammett (1894–1961) wrote five successful novels in as many years, including *The Maltese Falcon* (1930), then failed to produce anything else for the remaining twenty-seven years of his life. Harper Lee (1926–2016) was unable to follow up on her Pulitzer Prize-winning novel *To Kill a Mockingbird* (1960) – the so-called sequel *Go Set a Watchman*, written earlier but published fifty-five years later, now regarded as merely a first draft of her celebrated book.

Few cases of writer's block are more remarkable than that of the American novelist Henry Roth (1906–95). Roth's critically acclaimed first novel *Call It Sleep* was published in 1934. Then, sixty unproductive years later he published a second – *Mercy of a Rude Stream* – in four volumes (1994–98), the last two of them posthumously. The blockage well and truly unblocked.

CASH INCENTIVE

Anthony Trollope (1815–82) shocked his devoted readers when he revealed in *An Autobiography*, published a year after his death, that his principal motivation as a writer had been to make money. Trollope wrote forty-seven novels, several travel books, some short stories and a biography or two. An impressive output considering that for much of the time his day job was as a senior civil servant with the Post Office (he was largely responsible for the introduction of the pillar box). Among his best-known works are the 'Barsetshire' novels, chronicling the provincial lives of clergy and gentry, and his series of political novels featuring the Palliser family.

In his autobiography, Trollope records details of his publishing contracts and income with the exactitude of a lifelong civil servant. He also describes his daily writing routine, which began at 5.30 a.m. and included a self-imposed target of 250 words every fifteen minutes. He would typically complete forty manuscript pages a week – around 10,000 words – but occasionally would write over a hundred pages. Manuscripts always arrived on the publisher's desk on time.

TIME AND MOTION

The popular English author Arnold Bennett (1867–1931) kept track of his prolific output in his daily journal, which itself ran to over a million words. The entry for the last day of 1908, a typical year workwise, records that in the previous twelve months Bennett wrote two novels, a play, two self-improvement books, half-a-dozen short stories and over sixty articles for newspapers and magazines. 'Total words 423,500.'

TAKING DICTATION

The British novelist Barbara Cartland (1901–2000) dictated her bestselling romantic tales. Reclining on a sofa, with a fur draped over her legs and a hot-water bottle at her feet, and more often than not clutching one of her poodle dogs, she would create her stories aloud, the words diligently taken down in shorthand by her secretary. Since much of the text consisted of dialogue, Cartland felt that the spoken word would read more authentically on the page. Aiming to complete a chapter a day, she would generally finish a novel in under three weeks.

An altogether different writer, Henry James (1843–1916), took to dictating his books late in life. His amanuensis was Theodora Bosanquet, who worked alongside the distinguished American man of letters for nearly ten years. The author gave few clues regarding punctuation, which probably explains the labyrinthine structure of many of his sentences. Theodora Bosanquet went on to have her own literary career after James's death and took a keen interest in psychical research. She claimed to have communicated at a séance with the deceased authors George Meredith (1828–1909), Thomas Hardy (1840–1928) and John Galsworthy (1867–1933), along with Henry James himself, all of them in search of someone to take down their words from beyond the grave. Theodora obliged, compiling a sizeable archive of their spiritual outpourings – though there was no forwarding address for the royalties.

IT'S A FACT!

The reclusive American poet Emily Dickinson (1830–86) wrote nearly 1,800 poems, only six of which were published in her lifetime. Most of her poems can be sung to the tune of 'The Yellow Rose of Texas'.

NOVEL INDEX

Vladimir Nabokov (1899–1977) wrote the first nine of his fifteen novels in Russian, his native tongue. His family had fled revolutionary Russia in 1920, settling in Germany before making their way to the USA twenty years later. He came to international fame in 1955 with *Lolita*, which he wrote in English. The book's subject matter (see the chapter Ban the Book, page 37) led to it being initially prohibited in some countries.

Nabokov's novel-writing methodology was almost certainly unique. A flamboyant literary stylist whose narratives abound with wordplay and riddles, Nabokov wrote his books in pencil on lined index cards, which he would shuffle from time to time so that they appeared in no particular order. He would take up the narrative at different points in the story by selecting the appropriate card. Eventually, having sorted out the final running order of the cards (that is to say, the sequence of the story), Nabokov would hand them over to his wife Vera so that she could type the manuscript.

IT'S A FACT!

Anthony Burgess (1917–93), English novelist, screenwriter, librettist, literary critic, linguist and translator, whose best-known works include *A Clockwork Orange* (1962) and *Earthly Powers* (1980), also found time to write over 250 musical works, from piano pieces to full-blown symphonies.

VOX POP

Studs Terkel's (1912–2008) working day was different to that of most authors. For forty-five years, he had a daily show on the Chicago radio station WFMT, during which he conducted close to 9,000 taped interviews. Many of these were with famous visitors to the Windy City, but the majority were one-to-one conversations with members of the general public. Ordinary folk from all walks of life. Much of this recorded material was converted by Terkel into a series of critically acclaimed oral histories reflecting, often in a deeply personal way, aspects of the American way of life, past and present.

Division Street, published in 1967, chronicled the lives of seventy Chicagoans, separated by class and race. *Hard Times* (1970) focused on some of those who had survived the Great Depression. His 1974 book *Working* was all about just that. While in *The Good War* (1984), which earned Terkel a Pulitzer Prize, a cross section of American men and women recount their experiences during the Second World War. As much as the personal narratives themselves, it is Terkel's remarkable skill in shaping and linking the content that brings the topics vividly to life. As for his adopted first name, the writer-broadcaster owes that to another great Chicago character, Studs Lonigan, the eponymous hero of a fictional trilogy by James T. Farrell (1904–79). Terkel's parents, less adventurously, named him Louis.

CREATURE OF HABIT

Truman Capote (1924–84), author of *Breakfast at Tiffany's* (1958) and the 'non-fiction' novel (a story of real people and events told with the dramatic techniques of a novel) *In Cold Blood* (1966), described himself as a 'completely horizontal' writer. He always wrote in a recumbent position, in bed or on a couch. Early drafts of his novels or stories would be in longhand, and always on yellow paper. He would switch to a typewriter, balanced on his knees, to produce the final version of the manuscript. A highly superstitious man (he would change hotel rooms if the telephone number had

13 in it), Capote would never start or finish a piece of work
on a Friday for fear it would bring him bad luck.

PRODUCTIVITY RATES

Quantity is no guarantee of quality, but it can do wonders for
the income. Danielle Steel's name dominates the cover of millions
of paperbacks worldwide. The American novelist, born Danielle
Fernandes Dominique Schuelein-Steel in 1947, has written 129
books at the time of writing, including a dozen or so for children.
Since she publishes three books a year and works on several
at the same time, this figure is likely to be out of date before
this particular book goes to print. Her novels are on sale in
sixty-nine countries and in forty-three languages. With more
than 800 million copies sold, she is the world's bestselling living
author and currently stands fourth in the all-time list behind
Agatha Christie, William Shakespeare and Barbara Cartland.

Cartland's grand total of 723 blushingly romantic novels
(it was the heroines who blushed, though perhaps some of
her readers did too) will take some beating. In the 1970s, her
productivity rate was in excess of twenty novels a year. In 1978,
she was distracted by having to record an album of love songs
with the Royal Philharmonic Orchestra (she was seventy-seven
at the time) but still managed to pass on twenty new books to her
publishers. Undaunted by criticism of her work, the industrious
Cartland had the last word, leaving several manuscripts to be
published after her death in 2000.

James Patterson (1947–) is a one-man publishing industry.
The prolific American writer (born the same year as Danielle
Steel, his consort in popular fiction) has published around 150

books in the past forty years. He has several book series on the go at one time: the Alex Cross novels, NYPD Red and the Women's Murder Club among them. A passionate campaigner for literacy among the young, Patterson also writes for children and teenagers and is the first author to have been simultaneously No. 1 on the *New York Times* adult and children's bestseller lists. He has sold more than 350 million books worldwide and was the first to clock up a million eBook sales. To maintain his extraordinary rate of production, Patterson works with a number of co-writers who put together much of the text. Not that his readers care. The 'James Patterson' branding on the cover is enough to guarantee monster sales – as the former advertising executive is only too aware.

WORDS, WORDS, WORDS

No one knows exactly how many books London-born Charles Hamilton (1876–1961) wrote, since he used a number of pseudonyms, most of them long forgotten. The most famous of them is 'Frank Richards', creator of Billy Bunter and Greyfriars School, tales of which entertained generations of schoolboys (for the girls, Hamilton, as 'Hilda Richards', came up with *Bessie Bunter of Cliff House School*). In addition to books, Hamilton in his various guises wrote countless stories for magazines such as *The Gem* and *The Magnet*. Altogether it is estimated that he wrote around 100 million words, the equivalent of 1,200 average-sized novels.

AGE GAP

Daisy Ashford (1881–1972) was nine years old when she wrote *The Young Visitors, or Mr Salteena's Plan*, a sharply observed novella about the late-Victorian upper-class society in which her family lived. Written in an exercise book, complete with spelling mistakes, the young Daisy put the story aside and moved on to other things. The story resurfaced thirty years later and was passed on to Sir James Barrie, author of *Peter Pan,* via a mutual friend. The great man was so impressed with Daisy's childhood effort that he not only found a publisher for the story but contributed an introduction to the published version, which came out in 1919. The book remains a popular children's classic.

The English novelist Mary Wesley (1912–2002) was a late starter. Her first adult novel, *Jumping the Queue*, was published in 1983 when the author was seventy-one (a couple of children's books written in her late fifties were her only other published works). Over the next fifteen years she produced a further nine novels, amassing sales of over three million copies. Her most successful book was *The Camomile Lawn* (1984), a wartime family saga which like her first novel was adapted for television. Not the least surprising aspect of the Mary Wesley story was the explicit depiction of sex in her books. But then she was no ordinary seventy-year-old.

LOST GENERATION

According to Ernest Hemingway, it was the writer and art collector Gertrude Stein (1874–1946) who coined the phrase the 'lost generation' to describe the writers and artists who had come of age during the First World War. Many of them made their way to Paris (or had simply remained there) at the war's end, bringing together an extraordinary mix of creative talent, most of it hell-bent on experimentation.

In the world of literature alone, 1920s Paris saw the emergence of the *avant-garde* poets T. S. Eliot (1888–1965), Ezra Pound (1885–1972) and E. E. Cummings (1894–1962). Hemingway, who wrote evocatively about the period in his memoir *A Moveable Feast* (1964), was himself one of a line-up of aspiring American writers that included F. Scott Fitzgerald (1896–1940), William Faulkner (1897–1962), Thornton Wilder (1897–1975) and Henry Miller (1891–1980). The cost of living was ridiculously cheap, which was just as well since most of them had very little money, relying on handouts from the few that were well-heeled or on the occasional remittance from 'back home'. Regular meeting places (now tourist attractions) included the cafes Café de Flore and Les Deux Magots, and the Brasserie Lipp – all in St Germain-des-Près in the 6th arrondissement.

ADVICE FOR WRITERS

'Read, read, read. Read everything – trash, classics, good and bad, and see how they do it… Then write. If it is good, you'll find out. If it's not, throw it out the window.'
William Faulkner (1897–1962)

'Always carry a notebook… the short-term memory only retains information for three minutes; unless it is

committed to paper you can lose an idea for ever.'
Will Self (1961–)

'For Godsake, keep your eyes open. Notice what's
going on around you.'
William Burroughs (1914–97)

'Protect the time and space in which you write. Keep
everybody away from it, even the people who are
most important to you.'
Zadie Smith (1975–)

'Never use jargon words like "reconceptualise",
"demassification", "attitudinally", "judgementally".
They are hallmarks of a pretentious ass.'
David Ogilvy (1911–99)

'Interesting verbs are seldom very interesting.'
Jonathan Franzen (1959–)

'Don't use words too big for the subject. Don't say
"infinitely" when you mean "very"; otherwise you
will have no word left when you want to talk about
something really infinite.'
C. S. Lewis (1898–1963)

'Substitute "damn" every time you're inclined to write
"very"; your editor will delete it and the writing will
be just as it should be.'
Mark Twain (1835–1910)

'Never write about a place until you're away from it,
because it gives you perspective. Immediately after
you've seen something you can give a photographic

*description of it and make it accurate. That's good
practice, but it isn't creative writing.'*
Ernest Hemingway (1899–1961)

*'In the planning stage of a book, don't plan the
ending. It has to be earned by all that will go before it.'*
Rose Tremain (1943–)

'Be your own editor/critic. Sympathetic but merciless!'
Joyce Carol Oates (1938–)

*'Nothing you write, if you hope to be any good, will
ever come out as you first hoped.'*
Lillian Hellman (1905–84)

*'It's not wise to violate the rules until you know how
to observe them.'*
T. S. Eliot (1888–1965)

MAKING CRIME PAY

'Show me a man or woman who cannot stand mysteries and I will show you a fool.'
RAYMOND CHANDLER (1888–1959)

The American writer Edgar Allan Poe (1809–49) is generally regarded as the founding father of detective fiction. His first such story, *The Murders in the Rue Morgue* (1841), introduced C. Auguste Dupin, a *chevalier* (knight) in the *Légion d'honneur*, France's highest order of merit, and a man with exceptional powers of analysis and rational deduction. Ring any bells? Strip away the French connection and it could be a description of Sherlock Holmes. Dupin is the central character in two of the other Poe detective stories (he wrote four in all): *The Mystery of Marie Rogêt* (1842) and *The Purloined Letter* (1844). Poe also invented the device of a less intelligent sidekick, who admiringly narrates the case history. At the time Poe presciently created the genre, there were no detectives at Scotland Yard and few American police forces had an investigative arm.

Arthur Conan Doyle acknowledged Poe's pioneering contribution when he wrote of detective fiction: 'On this narrow path the writer must walk, and he sees the footmarks of Poe always in front of him.' The first to follow in Poe's footsteps was the French author Émile Gaboriau (1832–73), who wrote a number of crime novels. The main protagonist in Gaboriau's stories was a police officer called Monsieur Lecoq, a character he based on the legendary head of the French Sûreté (the first national police investigation bureau), Eugène François Vidoçq. A former criminal, the poacher-turned-gamekeeper Vidoçq was said to be a master of disguise – another strand in the make-up of Sherlock Holmes.

IT'S A FACT!

Sherlock Holmes wasn't the only famous fictional detective to live in Baker Street. Sexton Blake, who first appeared in print in 1893, resided at No. 252, on the opposite side of the road. Like his more illustrious neighbour, Blake has become a multimedia character, going from books and comic strips to radio, TV and movies.

ELEMENTARY DEDUCTION

Sherlock Holmes entered the crime scene in *A Study in Scarlet*, published in *Beeton's Christmas Annual* in 1887. The author, Arthur Conan Doyle (1859–1930), was twenty-eight with a struggling medical practice in Southsea, Hampshire. He was paid £25 for his literary effort, which initially went largely unnoticed. A second and more successful novel, *The Sign of the Four*, was published two years later, followed in rapid succession by six short stories. The great detective and his intrepid companion Dr Watson had truly arrived, and their creator could give up the day job.

The real-life model for Holmes was Dr Joseph Bell, who taught medicine at Edinburgh University when Conan Doyle was a student there. In his lectures, and at the local infirmary where he was a surgeon, Bell would impressively demonstrate his deductive skills, identifying a patient's trade or habits from clues that were unobserved by anyone else. Tall and thin, with a narrow aquiline nose and penetrating eyes, the professor was a dead ringer for the future sleuth. Naturally, it required more than this to form the fully-fleshed Sherlock Holmes, the finished article down to Doyle's creative imagination and storytelling technique.

Despite the fame and fortune it brought him, Holmes became a millstone around Doyle's neck. He wrote other kinds of novels and stories, but the public clamoured for more of the celebrated duo at 221b Baker Street. Having killed off the detective, he was forced to resurrect him by popular demand (even Edward VII, at whose hands he received a knighthood in 1902, was a fan). The last collection of stories, *The Case-Book of Sherlock Holmes*, appeared in 1927, three years before Doyle himself left the scene. For the record, Holmes never uttered the immortal words, 'Elementary, my dear Watson'.

IT'S A FACT!

E. W. Hornung (1866–1921), who created the fictional character Raffles, gentleman thief and renowned amateur cricketer, was the brother-in-law of Sir Arthur Conan Doyle.

CATHOLIC CRIME BUSTER

G. K. Chesterton (1874–1936) – the initials stand for Gilbert Keith – had a finger in almost every literary pie: novelist, biographer, poet, essayist, critic and journalist. He was equally renowned as a humorist and polemicist. Chesterton, who later became a Catholic convert, was the creator of Father Brown, an amateur detective who, unlike Sherlock Holmes, had a spiritual rather than scientific approach to crime-solving. Father Brown is a portly, untidy figure who habitually carries a black umbrella that matches his priestly garb.

In many of the fifty-odd stories (starting with 'The Blue Cross', published in 1910) the religious sleuth is up against Hercule Flambeau, a French master criminal and yet another master of disguise – though being six-foot-four (1.93m) in height sometimes proves a giveaway. Father Brown later converts Flambeau to the straight and narrow, and the Frenchman goes on to aid and abet the priest as a fellow detective.

IT'S A FACT!

Carolyn Keene, the credited author of the long-running series of Nancy Drew mysteries (published between 1930 and 2003), is a pseudonym for the dozen or so writers who actually wrote the books.

FOUR QUEENS

For several decades, beginning in the 1920s, British crime fiction was dominated by four female writers, often referred to as the 'Queens of Crime': Agatha Christie, Dorothy L. Sayers, Margery Allingham and Ngaio Marsh.

AGATHA CHRISTIE (1890–1976)

Although she didn't always please the critics, there is no doubting the reading public's enthusiasm for Agatha Christie's books. It is estimated that more than two billion copies have been sold, making her the bestselling novelist of all time. Half of these have been translated editions, an indication of her worldwide popularity. Altogether she wrote sixty-six detective novels, 150 short stories and twenty plays, including the world's longest-running production, *The Mousetrap*.

Her first novel was *The Mysterious Affair at Styles* (1920), a country house murder which introduced the Belgian detective Hercule Poirot, as well as Captain Hastings in the familiar role of the slow-witted companion, and the hapless Inspector Japp of Scotland Yard. Fastidious, meticulous and absurdly vain, Poirot solves crime after crime, unhindered by his idiosyncratic command of the English language. He dies on the job in the novel *Curtain*, published in 1975 (a year before the author's own death), though the story was actually written in 1940 with Christie unsure of surviving the war.

Christie's other popular sleuth is the elderly amateur Miss Marple, the subject of a dozen novels and some twenty short stories (compared to Poirot's thirty-three novels and fifty-plus stories). Jane Marple, a 'white-haired old lady with a gentle, appealing manner', puts her detective skills to good use in her village of St Mary Mead. Her last case, *Sleeping Murder*, was published in 1976, though as with Poirot's final *Curtain* the book had been written during the Second World War and presumably for the same reason. Unlike her Belgian counterpart, however, the indomitable Miss Marple is not killed off.

DOROTHY L. SAYERS (1893–1957)

Born in the Fens, the daughter of a vicar, Dorothy Leigh Sayers was one of the first women to graduate from Oxford University. She began her professional life as an advertising copywriter, switching to a full-time literary career when her detective novels began to make money. The central character in her books is Lord Peter Wimsey, an urbane amateur sleuth who investigates crime for his own amusement (Wimsey's second name is 'Death', the full name being Lord Peter Death Bredon Wimsey, and his family motto is 'As My Whimsy Takes Me'). His valet and former batman Bunter often helps out, as does Harriet Vane, a writer of detective stories who later becomes Lady Wimsey and is said to be based on Sayers herself.

The novels are elegantly written and ingeniously plotted. Among the best are *Strong Poison* (1930), *Murder Must Advertise* (1933) and *The Nine Tailors* (1934). Sayers, who also wrote religious plays and books on theology, spent her final years translating Dante's *Divine Comedy*. Some forty years after Sayers' death, Jill Paton Walsh completed the unfinished novel *Thrones, Dominations* (1998) and has since written three further Peter Wimsey-Harriet Vane murder mysteries.

MARGERY ALLINGHAM (1904–66)

Margery Allingham's first novel, an historical adventure called *Blackkerchief Dick*, was published when she was nineteen. She claimed that the story had been communicated to her by seventeenth-century pirates during a series of séances – a scenario better suited to her later crime fiction. *The Crime at Black Dudley* (1929) was her first detective novel, introducing in a supporting role Albert Campion, who would become the principal crime-solver.

Like Lord Peter Wimsey, Allingham's hero is a dilettante detective. Albert Campion is not his real name and his true identity is never revealed, though there are hints of an aristocratic background. The character is developed over the series of novels (about nineteen in all), shifting from an amiable man-about-town sleuth to a more serious investigator connected to counter-intelligence. Campion is assisted in some of his enquiries by his manservant, an ex-con with the magnificent name Magersfontein Lugg. Among the most popular mysteries are *Traitor's Purse* (1941), *More Work for the Undertaker* (1949) and *The Tiger in the Smoke* (1952).

NGAIO MARSH (1895–1982)

Born in New Zealand, Ngaio Marsh trained as an actress and later worked as a theatre director. Her debut novel, *A Man Lay Dead* (1934), introduced Chief Inspector Roderick Alleyn, the first of thirty-two novels featuring the Scotland Yard detective. Alleyn (pronounced 'Allen'), though a dedicated police officer, is another in the long line of gentleman detectives; Marsh named him after Alleyn's School in Dulwich, where her father had been a pupil. His background as the son of a baronet, educated at Eton and Oxford, sets him apart from his professional colleagues, but he has a good relationship with his loyal sidekick Sergeant Fox, whom he affectionately calls 'Brer Fox'.

Some of the novels are set in the theatre world (e.g. *Enter a Murderer*, 1935) and many of Marsh's characters are actors, musicians and painters, reflecting her own social milieu. One of them, an artist named Agatha Troy, becomes Alleyn's wife. In *Vintage Murder* (1937) and *Died in the Wool* (1945) the detective finds himself on the New Zealand crime beat, as the author returns to her roots.

ROYAL SUCCESSION

P. D. James (1920–2014) and Ruth Rendell (1930–2015) became the new 'queens' on the throne in the 1960s, launching the careers of two of crime fiction's most celebrated policemen. James's Chief Inspector Adam Dalgleish (he later rises to the rank of Commander) is the son of a vicar and a published poet; unfamiliar credentials in Scotland Yard. Rendell's Chief Inspector 'Reg' Wexford solves crime on his local rural patch.

Rendell was the more prolific of the two authors (there are twice as many Wexford stories as those featuring Adam Dalgleish) and her tally of fifty crime novels includes the psychological thrillers written under her own name and that of 'Barbara Vine'. P. D. James also created a female sleuth, Cordelia Gray, who first features in *An Unsuitable Job for a Woman* (1972), where Adam Dalgleish crosses over from his own series to meet her; there is a fleeting reference to her in a later Dalgleish novel, *A Taste for Death* (1986), but James resists the temptation to have them join forces. Both of these literary grandees ended up in the House of Lords, though politically apart: Baroness James to the right, Baroness Rendell to the left.

THE MAIGRET FILE

- France's most famous fictional detective, Inspector Jules Maigret, featured in seventy-five novels and twenty-eight short stories, the first of which was published in 1931 and the last forty-one years later – an average rate of two and a half Maigret investigations per year. According to Georges Simenon (1903–89), his creator, none of the novels took longer than eleven days to write and the first was actually completed in just four days.
- Of the 103 Maigret stories, sixty-four are set in Paris, thirty-three elsewhere in France and five in other countries.
- In *Les Mémoires de Maigret*, published in 1961, Georges Simenon and his sleuth swap roles. The detective, now retired and looking back over his long career, is ostensibly the author of the book and Simenon himself is one of the central characters.
- Simenon was twenty-six when he penned the first Maigret novel and sixty-eight when he finished the last. Although not written in chronological order, the age span of Maigret across the entire collection is twenty-six to sixty-eight, mirroring that of his creator.

- The first Maigret novel, *Pietr-le-Letton* (*The Strange Case of Peter the Lett*), was written in the Dutch seaport of Delfzijl, where in 1966 a statue of the detective was unveiled by the pipe-smoking author.
- Maigret and his wife, Louise, lived at 130 boulevard Richard Lenoir in the 11th arrondissement in Paris. It was a real address but the Maigrets' apartment was on a non-existent fourth floor.

IT'S A FACT!

Georges Simenon claimed to have made love to more than 10,000 women in his lifetime, 8,000 of them prostitutes. The writer, whose first full sexual encounter was at the age of twelve, maintained an average strike rate thereafter of three women a week. Any more and he might not have had time to write his 500 books.

PRIVATE EYES

The private investigator, an altogether tougher breed than the gentleman detective, is the dominant character in much of American crime fiction. There are many examples: from Rex Stout's (1886–1975) Nero Wolfe, who lives up to his creator's name by downing several quarts of beer a day, to Ross Macdonald's (1915–83) laconic Californian Lew Archer; from Mickey Spillane's (1918–2006) brutally sexist Mike Hammer to Robert B. Parker's (1932–2010) ex-boxer Spenser, whose first name is never revealed. However, two writers – and their private eyes – stand out above the fray.

DASHIELL HAMMETT

Dashiell Hammett (1894–1961) could have been a character in one of his own crime stories. At the age of twenty-one, he joined the Pinkerton detective agency where his assignments included working as a bodyguard and strike-busting at the Montana mines (his first big 'bust' was apprehending a man who had stolen a Ferris wheel). He made the imaginative leap to becoming a writer and produced his best work in the space of five years, from 1929 to 1934. With the character Sam Spade, the sardonic private eye in *The Maltese Falcon* (1929), Hammett put down a marker for others to follow. Nick Charles in *The Thin Man* (1934) has a lighter touch. A retired private detective, he is married to a rich, younger wife, Nora, and together they booze and wisecrack their way through the murder mystery. The 'Thin Man' in the title refers to the character Nick Charles is hired to find, not to the detective himself; though the subsequent series of *Thin Man* movies, starring the slimly debonair William Powell, led many to believe the opposite.

Hammett's crisp writing style and snappy dialogue lifted crime fiction into a different league, but the author died a broken man. Suffering from tuberculosis and the effects of a lifetime's hard drinking, he fell victim to the anti-Communist hysteria of post-war America, spending six months in jail for refusing to name names. His partner of many years was the playwright Lillian Hellman.

RAYMOND CHANDLER

The Chicago-born Chandler (1888–1959) was educated at London's Dulwich College, whose literary old boys include P. G. Wodehouse and C. S. Forester, creator of Captain Hornblower. An ex-journalist and sacked oil executive, he turned to writing pulp fiction (mostly for the crime magazine *Black Mask*) at the age of forty-five. Like his contemporary Dashiell Hammett, Chandler was an alcoholic, a condition which limited his output. He wrote seven novels, starting with *The Big Sleep* (1939), all narrated by Los Angeles private eye Philip Marlowe. Marlowe is a loner, a tough guy with largely hidden sensibilities. Against type, he plays chess (more often than not with himself as the opponent) and occasionally quotes T. S. Eliot and Robert Browning.

His brilliant use of language masks the fragility of some of the plots. When asked who had murdered the chauffeur in *The Big Sleep*, Chandler is said to have replied: 'Oh him – I forgot about him.' Two of the other stand-out books are *Farewell, My Lovely* (1940) and *The Long Goodbye* (1953). All but one of his novels have been adapted for cinema and television, some several times, but the written version remains the best.

TARTAN NOIR

The American hard school of crime fiction has influenced the Scottish genre known as Tartan Noir, a term said to have been coined in the 1990s by James Ellroy (author of *L.A. Confidential*) who referred to Ian Rankin as the 'King of Tartan Noir'. Gritty social themes combine with violent crime, often with an anti-hero at the centre of the story. Credit for kick-starting the genre, at least in its modern form, usually goes to William McIlvanney (1936–2015) and his novel *Laidlaw* (1977), the first of three featuring Detective Inspector Jack Laidlaw, whose bruising criminal patch is Glasgow.

Ian Rankin's (1960–) DI John Rebus is based in Edinburgh. A heavy drinker with a chaotic private life, Rebus is nevertheless a dab (if sometimes unsteady) hand at solving crimes and exposing corruption in the Scottish capital. Since Rebus's debut in *Knots and Crosses* (1987), Rankin has written a string of bestsellers featuring his flawed hero.

Although not all Val McDermid's (1955–) crime stories are set in Scotland, she can still be considered a fully paid-up member of the Tartan Noir club. The Scottish-born writer has a scatter approach to the genre, with a number of series on the go. The best known of them features criminal psychologist Dr Tony Hill and his police associate DCI Carol Jordan. Other McDermid protagonists include crime journalist Lindsay Gordon, a self-proclaimed 'socialist lesbian feminist'; Manchester private investigator Kate Brannigan; and DCI Karen Pirie, who is based in the Fife region, where the author herself was born.

SCANDINAVIAN BEAT

In recent years, the Scandinavian crime novel has become popular around the world. Henning Mankel (1948–2015) led the charge with his Kurt Wallander novels. The opera-loving Swedish cop, a loner who drinks too much (shades of Inspector Morse), has a lot of Bergmanesque angst in his life. So does Harry Hole from neighbouring Norway, the Oslo Crime Squad detective who is the hero of Jo Nesbø's (1960–) hugely successful thrillers. Hole smokes and drinks excessively and is in constant strife with his superiors. So no change there. Sweden's Stieg Larsson (1954–2004), an investigative journalist whose specialist subject was right-wing extremism, had planned to write a series of ten novels but had only completed three when he died of a heart attack. Published posthumously, *The Girl with the Dragon Tattoo* (2005), *The Girl Who Played with Fire* (2006) and *The Girl Who Kicked Over the Hornet's Nest* (2007) became known collectively as the Millennium trilogy.

PROFILING THE DETECTIVES

Enquiring amateurs
C. Auguste Dupin (Edgar Allan Poe)

Lord Peter Wimsey (Dorothy L. Sayers)

Philo Vance (S. S. Van Dine)

Ellery Queen (Ellery Queen)

Nancy Drew (Carolyn Keene)

Miss Marple (Agatha Christie)

Albert Campion (Margery Allingham)

Religiously inspired
Father Brown (G. K. Chesterton)

Brother Cadfael (Ellis Peters)

William of Baskerville (Umberto Eco)

Rabbi David Small (Harry Kemelman)

Sister Fidelma (Peter Tremayne)

Ex-nun Anne Fitzgerald (James Patterson)

Married partners
Thomas and Prudence Beresford (Agatha Christie)

Nick and Nora Charles (Dashiell Hammett)

Paul and Steve Temple (Francis Durbridge)

Mr and Mrs North (Frances and Richard Lockridge)

Thomas and Charlotte Pitt (Anne Perry)

Peter Decker and Rina Lazarus (Faye Kellerman)

Police pros
Charlie Chan (Earl Derr Biggers)

Roderick Alleyn (Ngaio Marsh)

Adam Dalgleish (P. D. James)

Dalziel and Pascoe (Reginald Hill)

Reginald Wexford (Ruth Rendell)

Endeavour Morse (Colin Dexter)

Hieronymus 'Harry' Bosch (Michael Connelly)

John Rebus (Ian Rankin)

Karen Pirie (Val McDermid)

Private eyes
Philip Marlowe (Raymond Chandler)

Sam Spade (Dashiell Hammett)

Mike Hammer (Mickey Spillane)

Hercule Poirot (Agatha Christie)

Cordelia Gray (P. D. James)

Spenser (Robert B. Parker)

Jackson Brodie (Kate Atkinson)

Precious Ramotswe (Alexander McCall Smith)

V. I. Warshawski (Sara Paretsky)

Forensic detailers
Sherlock Holmes (Arthur Conan Doyle)

Dr John Thorndyke (R. Austin Freeman)

Lincoln Rhyme (Jeffery Deaver)

Temperance Brennan (Kathy Reichs)

Dr David Hunter (Simon Beckett)

Kay Scarpetta (Patricia Cornwell)

Continental cops
Jules Maigret (Georges Simenon)

Piet Van der Valk (Nicolas Freeling)

Aurelio Zen (Michael Dibdin)

Kurt Wallander (Henning Mankel)

Salvo Montalbano (Andrea Camilleri)

Çetin Ikmen (Barbara Nadel)

Harry Hole (Jo Nesbø)

PRISON SENTENCES

'I wrote a million words in the first year, and I could never have done that outside of prison.'
JEFFERY ARCHER (1940-)

A surprising number of famous writers down the years have found themselves languishing in jail. With time on their hands, some took the opportunity to put pen to paper.

JOHN BUNYAN (1628-88)

Born in Bedfordshire, Bunyan was the son of a brazier (craftsman in brass) and learned to read and write in the village school. During the English Civil War, he fought for the Parliamentary side and later became a Baptist preacher. In 1660, with Charles II restored to the throne, Bunyan was arrested for preaching without a licence and spent most of the following twelve years in Bedford prison. He wrote nine books during his incarceration, including a part of *The Pilgrim's Progress* ('From This World to That Which Is to Come'), a Christian allegory and one of the most widely read works in the English language. Four years after being released from prison, Bunyan was briefly back inside, which gave him the opportunity to finish his masterpiece.

The first part of *The Pilgrim's Progress* was published in 1678, a second part following six years later.

JOHN CLELAND (1709-89)

After serving as the British consul in Smyrna (Turkey) and as the Bombay agent for the East India Company, John Cleland returned to London and fell on hard times. In 1748, he was sent to a debtors' prison and while there wrote *Fanny Hill, or the Memoirs of a Woman of Pleasure*. The titillating descriptions of the life of a prostitute, occasionally interrupted by some spurious moralising, made the book an instant bestseller when published the following year. The unfortunate Cleland missed out on the windfall, having sold the rights of the book for a flat fee of £20. *Fanny Hill* remained a classic of underground erotica for 200 years, until it was finally published in an unexpurgated version in 1963. Following an obscenity trial in the UK, the book was once again banned, only to be successfully republished seven years later.

IT'S A FACT!

Nazi leader Adolf Hitler (1889–1945) wrote the first part of his autobiography *Mein Kampf* (*My Struggle*) while in prison. Jailed after the failure of the so-called Munich Beer Hall Putsch in 1923, he dictated the text to his jack-booted aide Rudolf Hess.

MARQUIS DE SADE (1740-1814)

The notorious French nobleman, whose depraved activities gave us the word 'sadism', spent some thirty years of his life behind bars. His most famous book *Justine, or the Misfortunes of Virtue* (1791) was written while the author was serving time in the Bastille. The innocent Justine is sexually exploited and abused by just about everyone she comes across, sometimes at the instigation of her amoral sister Juliette, the eponymous heroine of a later Sade novel. Napoleon Bonaparte described *Justine* as the 'most abominable book ever engendered by the most depraved imagination' (he obviously hadn't read some of Sade's other works). Sade was finally committed to a mental asylum, almost certainly on a trumped-up diagnosis, where he spent the last thirteen years of his life. Reviled for many years after his death, the writer's work has been favourably reassessed in modern times.

LEIGH HUNT (1784-1859)

The English poet and essayist Leigh Hunt (in full, James Henry Leigh Hunt) was a prominent member of the Romanticism movement in England, which began in the late eighteenth century. Although not one of the great poets, he helped launch the careers of others such as John Keats and Percy Bysshe Shelley and, later, Robert Browning and Alfred Tennyson. As a journalist and critic, he co-founded with his brother John the influential weekly paper *The Examiner*. Following an editorial in which he described the Prince Regent (later George IV) as a 'fat Adonis of 50', he and his brother were jailed for two years and fined a hefty £500 apiece. It could have been worse. Hunt's family was allowed to live with him (his third child was born in prison), literary chums like Lord Byron and William Hazlitt could pop in for a chat, and there was a piano on hand for musical interludes. He was even allowed to continue editing *The Examiner*. It was while in prison that Hunt, despite the domestic distractions, wrote his major narrative poem *The Story of Rimini* (1816), a tragic tale of love inspired by Dante's *Inferno* (1320).

LAST-MINUTE REPRIEVE

On the morning of 22 December 1849, the 28-year-old Russian novelist Fyodor Dostoevsky was lined up in front of a firing squad in St Petersburg's Semenovsky Square. His alleged crime was reading and disseminating political material banned by the tsarist regime. Nineteen other political prisoners were about to share his fate. With mere moments to spare before the execution took place, a messenger arrived with a reprieve signed by the tsar. The death sentence was commuted to a term of imprisonment in the icy wastes of Siberia. Dostoevsky served four years' hard labour in a camp at Omsk, an experience he wrote about in *The House of the Dead* (1861).

OSCAR WILDE (1854-1900)

The Irish-born playwright, poet, essayist and wit, Oscar Fingal O'Flahertie Wills Wilde was the toast of London society with a string of successful plays that included *Lady Windermere's Fan* (1892) and *The Importance of Being Earnest* (1895). All that came to an end with his imprisonment for homosexuality in 1895, following a sensational trial. Sentenced to two years' punishing hard labour, Wilde still managed to pen a 50,000-word 'letter' to his friend Lord Alfred Douglas (his beloved 'Bosie') whose relationship with the writer had led to his downfall. Titled *De Profundis* (*Out of the Depths*), the first two words of Psalm 130, it is a moving blend of confession and reproach, published posthumously in 1905.

Wilde was released from prison in 1897 and fled to France. There he wrote 'The Ballad of Reading Gaol' (1898), a poetic indictment of the Victorian penal system. The poem was published under the pseudonym 'C.3.3' – the prisoner of Cell 3, third landing.

O. HENRY (1862–1910)

Born in North Carolina, William Sydney Porter was convicted in 1898 of embezzling funds from a Texas bank and sentenced to five years in prison (he was let out after three for good behaviour). Porter worked for a time in the prison pharmacy where the *U.S. Dispensatory* was an essential reference tool. Listed in the book was the French pharmacist Etienne-Ossian Henry – the probable inspiration for the nom de plume 'O. Henry' he used for several short stories he published while in jail. Stories gleaned from his fellow inmates were converted by the prolific writer into some of his most memorable tales.

IT'S A FACT!

The British philosopher and mathematician Bertrand Russell (1872–1970) was jailed for six months during the First World War for promoting pacifism. He put his period of incarceration to good use by writing his seminal work, *An Introduction to Mathematical Philosophy* (1919).

CHESTER HIMES (1909–84)

The black American crime writer Chester Himes got off to a bad start. In 1928, at the age of nineteen and a university student, he was sentenced to 'twenty to twenty-five years' in the Ohio State Penitentiary for stealing jewellery. Eight years into his term he was paroled. Himes's rehabilitation began with writing stories in prison, several of which were published, one in *Esquire* magazine. His first novel, *If He Hollers Let Him Go* (1948), is an impassioned account of racism in America. Himes himself, disgusted by the racial divisions in his country, became an exile in France and later Spain. Encouraged by a French publisher, he switched to crime fiction, setting his novels in the Harlem district of New York. In the process Himes created two of the most colourful characters in the entire genre, the black police detectives 'Coffin Ed' Johnson and 'Grave Digger' Jones. Funny, violent and fast-moving, the stories are played out on the streets of Harlem among the pimps and prostitutes, the dope pedlars and religious charlatans.

JEAN GENÊT (1910-86)

The French novelist and playwright started life as a professional thief, an activity which earned him several jail sentences. It was during one of these spells of incarceration that Genêt wrote his first novel, *Notre Dame des Fleurs* (*Our Lady of the Flowers*). The narrative centres on four individuals: Divine, a gay transvestite prostitute; Darling Daintyfoot, 'her' lover and pimp; Our Lady of the Flowers, a young murderer, later arrested and executed; and the author himself. The novel was first published anonymously in 1943 and circulated among collectors of erotica. No sooner had Genêt emerged from prison than he was arrested once again, this time for stealing books. Because of his repeated offending he faced a life sentence, but French cultural heavyweights including Jean-Paul Sartre, Jean Cocteau and Pablo Picasso rallied to his support – Cocteau telling the judge that Genêt was the 'greatest writer of the modern era'. The prisoner was released and never returned to jail again. A somewhat cleaned-up version of *Our Lady of the Flowers* appeared in 1951, to critical acclaim.

The American novelist Nelson Algren (1909–81) whose best-known work is *The Man with the Golden Arm* (1949), a landmark of post-war American literature, was jailed for five months as a young man for stealing a typewriter, on which he was learning his trade.

P. G. WODEHOUSE (1881–1975)

The creator of Bertie Wooster and Jeeves didn't go to prison, but was held in a German internment camp during the war. Wodehouse had been in the French resort of Le Touquet when the German Army arrived in 1940. He was arrested and subsequently transported to the camp in Tost, in Upper Silesia. His captors provided him with a typewriter and he used the time to write a novel, *Money in the Bank*, which was published first in America in 1942. A year after his arrest, Wodehouse was escorted by the Gestapo to Berlin where he unwisely (but perhaps understandably) agreed to do a series of light-hearted broadcasts for an American audience about his life as an internee. Wodehouse and his wife Ethel were then moved to Paris and installed by the Germans in a hotel, where they remained until the city was liberated in 1944. Despite the innocuous nature of the broadcasts, Wodehouse's actions caused an outcry in Britain. He was accused of being a traitor. Some libraries removed his books from the shelves, though fellow writers incuding George Orwell and Evelyn

Waugh spoke out in his defence. Wodehouse settled in the USA, becoming an American citizen in 1955. In 1975 he was knighted, all presumably forgiven.

JEFFREY ARCHER (1940–)

In 2001, politician-turned-bestselling-novelist Jeffrey Archer was sentenced to four years in prison for perjury and perverting the course of justice. In the event, he served only half the sentence, but it was time enough in which to produce a diary in three volumes, named after the three parts of Dante's *The Divine Comedy*: 'Hell', 'Purgatory' and 'Heaven'. *Hell* (2002) records the author's stay of twenty-two days and fourteen hours in Her Majesty's Prison Belmarsh, a high-security jail in south London and home to some of Britain's most violent criminals. Archer then spent sixty-seven days in HMP Wayland, a medium-security establishment in Norfolk, the subject of *Purgatory* (2003). In the final book of *A Prison Diary*: *Heaven* (2004), prisoner FF8282 is confined to the more agreeable North Sea Camp in Lincolnshire, a 'Category D' open prison – though he experiences a brief return to harsher conditions in Lincoln jail, following a breach of home-visit regulations. Finally, the author (and his readers) are released.

IT'S A FACT!

In 1954, two New Zealand schoolgirls murdered the mother of one of them (a story told by Peter Jackson in his 1994 film *Heavenly Creatures*). After serving time in prison, one of the girls, Juliet Hulme, moved to the UK and later became a writer, publishing more than forty mystery novels under the name Anne Perry.

📚 BOOK OF 📚 THE MONTH: A NOVEL SELECTION

Doctor January (Rhoda Baxter, 2014)

Summer in February (Jonathan Smith, 1995)

March: A Love Story in a Time of War (Geraldine Brooks, 2005)

April Lady (Georgette Heyer, 1957)

The Darling Buds of May (H. E. Bates, 1958)

The Ides of June (Rosemary Rowe, 2016)

The Twelfth Day of July (Joan Lingard, 1970)

August 1914 (Alexander Solzhenitsyn, 1971)

September (Rosamunde Pilcher, 1990)

The Hunt for Red October (Tom Clancy, 1984)

Butterflies in November (Audur Ava Ólafsdóttir, 2004)

A Week in December (Sebastian Faulks, 2009)

FAMILY CONNECTIONS

'One day I will write verses about him and see how he likes it.'

**CHRISTOPHER MILNE (1920-96)
ABOUT HIS FATHER, A. A. MILNE**

Writing is often a family affair, a pursuit shared by spouses or partners, by siblings, or across generations, though sometimes with differing degrees of critical or commercial success.

LAMBS' TALES

Charles Lamb (1775–1834) was a schoolmate of the poet Samuel Taylor Coleridge, both attending Christ's Hospital (a.k.a. the Bluecoat School) in the City of London. Later literary friends included William Wordsworth, William Hazlitt and Leigh Hunt. Noted for his generosity of spirit, Lamb's life was nevertheless marked by frustration and tragedy. A stammer prevented him from going to university so he was forced to work as a clerk with the East India Company. As a writer he is best known for his collected essays, *The Essays of Elia*, written between 1820 and 1825. One of the most famous is 'A Dissertation upon Roast Pig', a humorous account about cooking pork.

He collaborated with his older sister Mary (1764–1847) on *Tales from Shakespeare* (1807), prose versions of the plays that are still read by children today. A strain of insanity ran in the Lamb family and Mary had several bouts of madness, during one of which she stabbed her mother to death. Charles took on the responsibility of caring for his sister, but died twelve years before she did – by coincidence in the same year as his lifelong friend Coleridge.

FUNERAL EXPENSES

Samuel Johnson (1709–84) wrote his only novel, *The History of Rasselas, Prince of Abyssinia* (1759), in order to pay for his ninety-year-old mother's funeral and to settle her debts. The book, a philosophical romance, is said to have been written over the course of a single week. In essence, it debunks the idea that a state of true happiness can be attained through some simple formula, such as going back to nature – a popular notion in the eighteenth century. Whether or not the message was heeded, the novel proved a success and quickly earned Johnson the necessary funds.

LITERARY CONSEQUENCES

It was at a publisher's dinner party in London in 1791 that the feminist writer Mary Wollstonecraft (1759–97) first met novelist and philosopher William Godwin (1756–1836). Other guests at the distinguished gathering included the revolutionary Tom Paine, author of *The Rights of Man* (1792), and poets William Blake, Samuel Taylor Coleridge and William Wordsworth. Wollstonecraft and Godwin didn't see eye to eye and it would be another four years before they met again; after which they became lovers.

Wollstonecraft's groundbreaking work, *A Vindication of the Rights of Woman*, had been published in 1792. Godwin was already established as one of the foremost philosophers of his day; he had also written a remarkably 'modern' novel, *The Adventures of Caleb Williams* (1794), part social commentary, part whodunnit. When Wollstonecraft became pregnant the couple married, though characteristically for two highly independent individuals, they maintained separate homes. The child, Mary, was born in August 1797. But the couple's happiness was short-lived, the mother dying of septicaemia little more than a week later.

In 1814, at the age of seventeen, Mary Godwin eloped abroad with the poet Percy Bysshe Shelley (1792–1822). When Shelley's first wife died two years later, the runaway pair married. During their brief time together, Mary Shelley wrote her iconic novel *Frankenstein, or the Modern Prometheus* (1818). Following Shelley's death in 1822, Mary returned to England with their son Percy junior. She never remarried and died in 1851.

IT'S A FACT!

The Scarborough-born Sitwell siblings – Dame Edith Sitwell (1887–1964), Sir Osbert Sitwell (1892–1969) and Sacheverell Sitwell (1897–1988) – were prolific contributors to the British cultural scene with poetry, biography, history, art criticism, travel books and fiction.

THREE SISTERS

The Brontë story is a classic tale of triumph over adversity. The three Brontë sisters – Charlotte, Emily and Anne – along with their brother Branwell (his mother's maiden name), were brought up by their widowed father, an Irish curate. The family lived in the parsonage at Haworth, a village on the edge of the West Yorkshire moors. Two elder sisters died of tuberculosis in 1825 and all the remaining children were dogged by ill health. The wild moorland nearby was a stimulant to the children's imaginations. Charlotte and Branwell created a fantasy African empire, which they named Angria. Emily and Anne conjured up an imaginary world called Gondal. It was all a rehearsal for the real thing.

In 1846, the three sisters published a volume of poetry as Currer, Ellis, and Acton Bell – the pseudonyms of Charlotte (1816–55), Emily (1818–48) and Anne (1820–49) respectively, and names they would use throughout their brief writing careers. The following year produced a trio of novels: Charlotte's *Jane Eyre*, which drew on her experiences at boarding school and as a governess; Emily's *Wuthering Heights*, her only novel and considered by many to be the finest Brontë work; and Anne's *Agnes Grey*. Tragedy trailed their success. Emily died in 1848, having caught a chill at her brother Branwell's funeral. Anne published one more novel, *The Tenant of Wildfell Hall*, in 1849, the year of her own death. Charlotte, stripped of her beloved siblings, wrote two more novels, *Shirley* (1849) and *Villette* (1853). She died in 1855 at the age of thirty-eight. Her first fictional work, *The Professor*, was published posthumously in 1857.

FAMILY HORROR STORY

Alfred, Lord Tennyson (1809–92), whose poetry wooed and inspired the Victorian public, was the fourth son of twelve children. His father, rector of a parish in Lincolnshire, was mentally unstable, took to drink and drugs and on one occasion tried to kill Arthur's elder brother Frederick. Of the other children, one was confined to an asylum for much of his life, another was a drug addict, a third an alcoholic. A fourth died young, having been committed intermittently to a mental institution. Several of the remaining offspring were manic depressives (unsurprisingly) or subject to bouts of religious mania. The mother of this unhappy brood, Elizabeth, suffered additionally from the maltreatment of her brutal husband. Yet from this relentlessly grim environment emerged some of the most revered poetry in the English language.

MARRIAGE LINES

Robert Browning (1812–89) and Elizabeth Barrett (1806–61) admired each other's poetry before they got to admire each other. Writing to thank Miss Barrett for her favourable review of his *Dramatic Lyrics* (1842), Browning requested to call on her. After a clandestine courtship lasting four years (Barrett's tyrannical father disapproved of Browning, along with any other suitors), the couple sneaked off to St Marylebone Parish Church in London and were married. Barrett returned to the family home in nearby Wimpole Street for a week, keeping her new status a secret. The couple then took off for a fresh life in Italy.

The poetic partnership was fruitful. Elizabeth Barrett Browning's *Sonnets from the Portuguese* (1850) and the blank-verse novel *Aurora Leigh* (1857) are rated among her finest works. Browning produced *The Ring and the Book* (1869), a monumental poem in blank verse comprising 21,000 lines and originally published in twelve volumes. The poem, based on an actual seventeenth-century Italian murder case, is narrated by twelve characters (each a separate volume). The couple lived contentedly in Italy for fifteen years until, in the best romantic tradition, Elizabeth died in the arms of her husband.

WEDDING VOW

In 1935, the British poet W. H. Auden (1907–73) married Erika Mann, daughter of the Nobel Prize-winning German novelist Thomas Mann (*The Magic Mountain*, *Death in Venice*, etc.) so that she could escape from Nazi Germany on a UK passport. They met for the first time on their wedding day and never spent a night together. It was all the idea of Auden's friend, the writer Christopher Isherwood, a homosexual like Auden. Although Auden went on to share his life with his long-time companion Chester Kallman, his marriage to Erika Mann remained intact until her death in 1969.

FATHER AND SON

Alexandre Dumas (1802–70) was born in northern France, his father of mixed race from what is now Haiti. He started out as a journalist and playwright, before turning to fiction. A man of tremendous energy, he did everything to excess. At the time of his death his literary output totalled close to 300 books. He earned vast sums of money, which he lavishly spent, and is said to have had forty mistresses – though presumably not at the same time. He employed a team of collaborators (he called them his 'factory') to plunder earlier published works for usable plots and characters. His swashbuckling historical romances were hugely popular, the best of them becoming enduring classics – *The Three Musketeers* (1844), *Twenty Years After* (1845), in which D'Artagnan and his three fellow swordsmen are reunited, and *The Count of Monte Cristo* (1846).

One of his many romantic liaisons produced an illegitimate son who also became a writer, confusingly sharing the same name of Alexandre Dumas (1824–95). To keep them distinct, the two are normally referred to as Dumas *père* ('father') and Dumas *fils* ('son'). Although he wrote more than a dozen novels, the younger Dumas is best known as a popular playwright. His most famous dramatic work is the 1848 play *La Dame aux Camelias* (*The Lady of the Camellias*), which Verdi turned into the opera *La Traviata* and Greta Garbo into her most celebrated screen role as *Camille*.

IT'S A FACT!

Readers of his classic tales may be surprised to know that Alexandre Dumas, *père*, was also the author of *Grand Dictionnaire de Cuisine*, a highly respected cookbook and culinary encyclopaedia. The book was published posthumously in 1873, three years after the writer's last meal.

WRITING DYNASTY

The Waugh family had its roots in Somerset. Arthur Waugh (1866–1943) was a literary critic and biographer (he wrote the first biography of the poet Alfred, Lord Tennyson) and a successful London publisher. Even more importantly, he was the father of Alec and Evelyn.

Alec (1898–1981), the older of the two brothers, came to prominence with his novel *The Loom of Youth* (1917), published when the author was only nineteen. The book, a semi-autobiographical exposé of public school life, with undercurrents of homosexuality, became a controversial bestseller. Alec Waugh went on to write a number of popular novels, the best known of which is *Island in the Sun* (1955), later a film with a starring role and hit song for Harry Belafonte.

Evelyn Waugh (1903–66) was one of Britain's finest twentieth-century novelists. He made his mark with early satirical works such as *Decline and Fall* (1928), *Vile Bodies* (1930) and *Scoop* (1938), a masterly send-up of war reporting. His wartime experiences (some of which took place in Crete and Yugoslavia, where he was sent to liaise with the Communist partisans) led to *Put Out More Flags* (1942) and the tragi-comic *Sword of Honour* trilogy (1952–1961). Other novels include *Brideshead Revisited* (1945) – the trials and tribulations, spiritual and otherwise, of an aristocratic Roman Catholic family (Waugh himself was a Catholic convert) – and *The Loved One* (1948), a black comedy about Californian funeral practices.

Auberon Waugh (1939–2001), son of Evelyn, was a brilliant and outspoken journalist, whose satirical diary in *Private Eye* magazine ran for over a decade. As editor of the *Literary Review*, he co-founded the 'Bad Sex in Fiction Award', targeting redundant or ill-written sexual descriptions. His own five novels suffered in comparison with those of his father. Two of Auberon's children have taken the family business into a fourth generation: Daisy Waugh (1967–) is a novelist; Alexander Waugh (1963–) is the author of *Fathers and Sons* (2007), a biography of his literary family.

MOTHER AND DAUGHTER

American bestselling writer Jodi Picoult (1966–) has written over twenty novels, the first of which was *Songs of the Humpback Whale*, published in 1992. One day her fourteen-year-old daughter, Samantha van Leer, pitched her an idea for a young-adult novel, a genre the author had not previously ventured into. They decided to collaborate and the result was *Between the Lines* (2012): the story of a young girl whose lonely existence is transformed when a handsome young prince steps off the page of the book she is reading and walks into her life. Following its success, mother and daughter produced a sequel, *Off the Page* (2015), featuring the same characters.

CHIP OFF THE BLOCK

Kingsley and Martin Amis, father and son, are two of the most outstanding British novelists of the past sixty years, both also producing major works of literary criticism. Kingsley Amis (1922–95) burst onto the literary scene with his 1954 novel *Lucky Jim*. A witty satire about academic life at an English university, the book's anti-hero Jim Dixon became a standard-bearer for the 'Angry Young Man' movement of the day. Amis senior, who also published volumes of poetry, went on to write another twenty-four novels, picking up the Booker Prize (in 1986, for *The Old Devils*) and a knighthood along the way. His youthful rebelliousness morphed into middle-aged grumpiness as he moved from left to right on the political spectrum.

Martin Amis's first novel, *The Rachel Papers* (1973), was published when the author was twenty-four (eight years faster than Kingsley's debut). The book successfully launched a writing career that has won plaudits and awards and considerable sales, but has not been without controversy. The themes of his sometimes violent novels, his experimentation with language and structure, and his outspoken social and political views have all attracted criticism. But a new Martin Amis book is always an event.

PARTNERS IN CRIME

In the 1960s, Swedish publisher Maj Sjöwall (1935–) and journalist Per Wahlöö (1926–75) became romantically involved. Both had been married before, Sjöwal twice. They moved in together and embarked on a series of ten novels, centred around detective Martin Beck of Stockholm's National Homicide Department. The first of them, *Roseanna*, was published in 1965. The collaborators' method of working was to write alternate chapters, with a formulaic thirty chapters per book. All ten novels became bestsellers and have been adapted for television and cinema. The private and professional partnership came to an end with the death of Per Wahlöö in 1975, just as their final book was going to print.

TEN FEMINIST BOOKS

A Vindication of the Rights of Women (1792)
Mary Wollstonecraft
An argument for equality

My Own Story (1914)
Emmeline Pankhurst
A suffragette's tale

A Room of One's Own (1929)
Virginia Woolf
Carving out some intellectual space

The Feminine Mystique (1963)
Betty Friedan
Housewives, throw off your shackles

Sexual Politics (1970)
Kate Millett
Feminist literary criticism

The Female Eunuch (1970)
Germaine Greer
Sexual liberation for women

Fat Is a Feminist Issue (1978)
Susie Orbach
The psychology of female dieting

The Beauty Myth (1991)
Naomi Wolf
Fighting female stereotypes

Feminism Is for Everybody (2000)
bell hooks
Exploring the nature of feminism

How to Be a Woman (2011)
Caitlin Moran
Feminist and fun

UNDER THE INFLUENCE

An addiction to drink or drugs, in some instances both, is the price many writers have paid for their creativity – the stimulants are used as a means of liberating the creative spirit or to smother the fear of failure. Some remarkable works have emerged under the influence.

GREEN FAIRY

Absinthe became the fashionable drink among writers and artists in France during the mid-nineteenth century. Called the 'Green Fairy' because of its colour and hallucinatory properties, the anise-flavoured, wormwood-based drink was highly alcoholic and addictive. Such was its popularity in the bars and cafes of Paris that the hour between five and six p.m. was known as *l'heure verte* ('the green hour'). The Green Fairy's destructive side effects, which included mind-shattering hallucinations and sudden blackouts, were often the result of downing a dozen or so powerful shots a day.

As LSD would do a century later, however, absinthe fired the imagination. The French symbolist poets Paul Verlaine (1844–96) and Arthur Rimbaud (1854–91) were enthusiastic imbibers, happily transported by the visionary spin-offs induced by the drink. So too was fellow poet Charles Baudelaire (1821–67) who used absinthe as well as opium, and in his poem 'Le Poison' ('The Poison') puts its effects ahead of those of wine and his favourite drug. Novelist Émile Zola (1840–1902) was another regular consumer of the spirit. Non-French followers of the colourful fairy included Oscar Wilde (1854–1900), James Joyce (1882–1941) and Ernest Hemingway (1899–1961). Hemingway created a cocktail called 'Death in the Afternoon' (the title of his 1932 celebration of bull-fighting), which combines absinthe and champagne and the recipe for which ends with the words: 'Drink three to five of these slowly.' He might have added, 'If you can'.

AMERICAN DISEASE

More than their British or European counterparts, American writers have plenty of form when it comes to the 'demon drink'. Five Nobel Prize laureates were alcoholics: Sinclair Lewis (who won the prize in 1930), Eugene O'Neill (1936), William Faulkner (1949), Ernest Hemingway (1954) and John Steinbeck (1962). To that distinguished number can be added, in the twentieth century alone, F. Scott Fitzgerald, Thomas Wolfe, Dashiell Hammett, Raymond Chandler, Dorothy Parker, John O'Hara, John Cheever, Raymond Carver, Tennessee Williams, Robert Lowell, Carson McCullers, James Jones, Truman Capote…

Alcohol certainly contributed to the demise of Edgar Allan Poe (1809–49), whose tragic life ended when he was forty. Poe spent his last few days in a drunken stupor, stumbling about the streets of Baltimore during an election and trying to cadge a drink in exchange for his vote. Jack London (1876–1916), best known for his classic canine tales *The Call of the Wild* (1903) and *White Fang* (1906), was a man of adventure, a former sailor, hobo and goldminer – but always with a bottle close at hand. In his autobiographical novel *John Barleycorn*, published three years before his death, London describes his long-term struggle with alcoholism.

For many successful or aspiring writers, consuming alcohol in large measure was a badge of honour. It went with the territory. William Faulkner (1897–1962), one of America's greatest-ever authors, once said: 'The tools I need for my work are paper, tobacco, food, and a little whiskey.' In fact, throughout his career Faulkner drank copious amounts of the spirit (though rarely while in the process of writing) and would go on benders lasting several days, at the end of which he was frequently hospitalised. As with most of those mentioned, alcoholism brought his life to a premature end.

IT'S A FACT!

The short-story writer O. Henry (1862–1910) drank an average of two quarts (1.9 litres) of whiskey per day. Despite this he maintained a healthy work rate, with over 600 stories published. A lifetime sufferer from hypoglycaemia, he once summed up his condition: 'I was born eight drinks below par.'

THE GREAT FITZGERALD

No writer's career was more publically scuppered by drink than that of F. Scott Fitzgerald (1896–1940). His first novel, *This Side of Paradise* (1920), sold 20,000 copies in the first week, and Fitzgerald and his beautiful wife Zelda embraced the jazz age to the full, carousing and partying away the nights (and frequently the days). When sober, the writer dedicated himself to recording the spirit of the times in print, but all too often the fun and games took over. Drink undermined Zelda's already unstable mental condition and she was eventually diagnosed as a schizophrenic. Fitzgerald tried to make light of his own increasing reliance on bootlegged booze by jokingly introducing himself to people with the words: 'Pleased to meet you – you know I'm an alcoholic.' The couple drank their way from New York to Paris and then to the French Riviera.

Fitzgerald completed just four novels, the most famous of which is *The Great Gatsby* (1925). The author himself considered *Tender Is the Night* (1934), his most ambitious novel and during his lifetime a commercial failure, to be his finest; though he confessed that it had been written 'entirely on stimulant'. A fifth, *The Last Tycoon*, which drew on the author's final years in Hollywood (off the drink at last but having to survive on hack screenwriting assignments), remained unfinished at his death, at the age of forty-four. Fitzgerald also wrote a considerable body of short stories, some of which – such as 'The Diamond as Big as the Ritz' – are among the finest in American literature.

VICIOUS CIRCLE

In the 1920s, the owner of the Algonquin Hotel in New York installed a large round table in the Rose Room to cater for a group of young writers and newspaper columnists who regularly met there. The Round Table became synonymous with the sharp, snappy humour of the Roaring Twenties, producing famous one-liners like 'Let's get out of these wet clothes and into a dry Martini.' Key members of the group included the writer and critic Dorothy Parker (1893–1967), playwright George S. Kaufman (1889–1961), novelist Edna Ferber (1885–1968), short story writer Ring Lardner (1885–1933), critic and essayist Alexander Woollcott (1887–1943) and writer-humorist Robert Benchley (1889–1945).

Their own name for this literary collective was the Vicious Circle, with verbal sparring an essential part of the action. One day at lunch, Dorothy Parker was challenged by her Round Table companions to come up with a sentence that contained the word 'horticulture', but not in its normal context. Her swift response was: 'You can lead a whore to culture, but you can't make her think.'

OPIUM MEMORIES

Opium was cheap and easy to buy in Britain in the early nineteenth century. Widely used as a painkiller and sedative, typically in the form of laudanum, it could be bought over the counter at chemists without a prescription. Unaware of its addictive properties, many of those who took it purely for medicinal purposes became hooked on the drug. The poet Samuel Taylor Coleridge (1772–1834) struggled with his addiction for many years. He claimed that his great poem 'Kubla Khan' (1797) had been composed during an opium-induced sleep, the lines written down immediately on waking. Other writers who became addicts include the poet George Crabbe (1754–1832) and novelist Wilkie Collins (1824–89).

Thomas De Quincey (1785–1859) was a friend of Coleridge, though they later fell out. An essayist and critic of note, he began to take opium to relieve a persistent and painful rheumatic condition. In his best-known book, *Confessions of an English Opium-Eater* (1822), De Quincey graphically describes his descent into addiction, contrasting the 'pleasures' of the drug with the 'pains'. The book also gives a shocking glimpse of the degradation and poverty in the London slums of the time. It made De Quincey's name and earned him serious money, much of which he gave away to beggars.

IT'S A FACT!

Aldous Huxley (1894–1963), English author of the futuristic novel *Brave New World* (1932), experimented with the hallucinatory drug mescaline, a natural product of the spineless cactus plant peyote. He describes the enhancing effects of the drug in his non-fiction work, *The Doors of Perception* (1954).

BEAT GENERATION

The predominantly male beat movement emerged in mid-1950s America, a part-social, part-cultural rejection of middle-class conformity and commercialism. Jazz, sexual freedom and drugs were the name of the game. The most prominent literary 'beatniks' were Jack Kerouac (1922–69), Allen Ginsberg (1926–97) and William S. Burroughs (1914–97). It was Kerouac who coined the phrase 'beat generation', with the blessed state of 'beatitude' in mind. Others chose to associate it with the ubiquitous jazz beat or to a dead-beat weariness with the status quo. His picaresque novel *On the Road* (1957) was written in three weeks in 1951, with the author stoked up on Benzedrine. He typed the words onto a lengthy roll of tracing paper, which he referred to as the 'scroll'. It took Kerouac six years to find a publisher but the book's immediate success prompted two further novels in quick succession; *The Subterraneans* and *The Dharma Bums* were both published in 1958.

Allen Ginsberg's 1956 collection *Howl and Other Poems*, with its homosexual fantasies and drug-inspired visions, became the subject of a landmark court case brought on the grounds that the book was obscene. The literary establishment (ironically, often the target of the beat movement) rallied to the cause and the charge was thrown out. The book's notoriety didn't harm sales. *Howl* was reprinted nineteen times over the next ten years, and today Ginsberg is recognised as one of the most influential poets of the post-war era.

William S. Burroughs's novel *Naked Lunch* (1959) was published first in Paris to avoid a head-on collision with America's obscenity laws. A loosely, even randomly structured work, its central character is William Lee, a junkie and the author's alter ego (Burroughs himself was addicted to heroin and morphine, among other substances). The drug-and-sex-fuelled text shocked many readers, but the book contains some brilliantly written passages and in places is very funny, though perhaps not always intentionally. Burroughs wrote much of *Naked Lunch* while living in Tangier, where he was joined briefly by Kerouac and Ginsberg who helped with the typing.

HORROR STORY

America's master of horror and the supernatural, Stephen King (1947–), has published more than fifty novels (half a dozen or so as Richard Bachman) and close to 200 short stories. His global sales top 350 million copies. Many of the works have spun off into films, television series and comic books. Yet for much of the

1980s King was a drug addict and alcoholic, though amazingly still able to churn out bestsellers.

By his own calculation, King would get through a case of beer each night, though he didn't normally drink and write. Cocaine was a different matter. Novels such as *Pet Sematary* (1983) and *Misery* (1987) were written when the author was heavily using the drug during the working day. Such was the combined effect of the drink and drugs, King claims to have no recollection about working on some of the books that eventually made it into the bestseller lists.

HIGH JINKS

Hunter S. Thompson (1937–2005) catapulted to fame with his cult classic *Fear and Loathing in Las Vegas*, published in 1972. The novel, subtitled 'A Savage Journey to the Heart of the American Dream', documents an anarchic drug-crazed road trip taken by journalist Raoul Duke and his attorney Dr Gonzo (the two characters are based on Hunter S. Thompson himself and his attorney friend Oscar Zeta Acosta). The book gave rise to the genre of 'gonzo journalism', a frenetic blend of fact and fiction with the reporter as part of the story. Thompson, who made no secret of his heavy drinking and drug taking, committed suicide at the age of sixty-seven. His most famous quote could be his epitaph: 'I hate to advocate drugs, alcohol, violence, or insanity to anyone, but they've always worked for me.' The 'S', by the way, stands for Stockton.

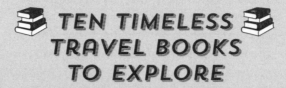

TEN TIMELESS TRAVEL BOOKS TO EXPLORE

The Innocents Abroad (1869)
Mark Twain

Arabian Sands (1959)
Wilfred Thesiger

Venice (1960)
Jan Morris

Travels with Charley: In Search of America (1962)
John Steinbeck

As I Walked Out One Midsummer Morning (1969)
Laurie Lee

The Great Railway Bazaar (1975)
Paul Theroux

In Patagonia (1977)
Bruce Chatwin

A Time of Gifts (1977)
Patrick Leigh Fermor

Coasting (1986)
Jonathan Raban

Epic Drives of the World (2017)
Lonely Planet

DEAR DIARY

'To be a good diarist one must have a little, snouty, sneaky mind.'
HAROLD NICOLSON (1886-1968)

Diaries are what you make them. Tony Benn's multi-volume epic (scaled down from the original 20 million words) is a meticulous record of a long political life. Actor Kenneth Williams's diary is a catalogue of woe and a spiteful attack on his fellow professionals. Housewife Nellie Last's daily account of life in Lancashire during the Second World War is moving and defiant. King George V's journal leaves a lot to be desired: 'It rained today, harder than yesterday: I hope it will not rain tomorrow.'

INSIDE PEEPS

Samuel Pepys (1633–1703) was twenty-seven when he commenced his famous diary on 1 January 1660. The son of a London tailor, he would eventually rise to become Secretary for Admiralty Affairs and a Member of Parliament, though at the start of the journal he is a clerk in the employ of his patron the Earl of Sandwich. The diary was written in shorthand, with no thought of publication. In its original form it comprises six leather-bound volumes, now housed in the Pepys Library at Magdalene College, Cambridge, the diarist's alma mater.

The period covered by the diary is a little over nine years, Pepys drawing a line under it on 31 May 1669 in the mistaken belief that he was going blind. The uninhibited entries give a remarkable insight not just into the big events of the day and the political manoeuvrings of his contemporaries, but also into seventeenth-century domestic life and the concerns of the ordinary citizen. Pepys was a star witness to both the Great Plague of 1665 and the Great Fire that wiped it out a year later. He also faithfully recorded (25 October 1668) his wife's discovery of him in flagrante with her companion Deborah Willet, leaving little to the reader's imagination. But then, he didn't know anyone else would read it – and they didn't, until 1825 when the diary was deciphered and first published (in part). It would be another 150 years before Pepys's sexual adventures made their way into print, earlier editors of the diary believing the text too explicit for publication.

OUT OF THE SHADOW

Separated for much of their childhood from her slightly older brother William, Dorothy Wordsworth (1771–1855) moved in with the poet in 1795 and shared a home with him until William's death fifty-five years later, remaining under the same roof even when William married Mary in 1802. For much of this time Dorothy kept a series of journals, starting with their brief sojourn in Somerset where they lived close to their friend, fellow poet Samuel Taylor Coleridge. In 1799, the Wordsworths moved to the Lake District – to Dove Cottage in Grasmere – with Dorothy recording details of her brother's working habits and of the stunning landscape that surrounded them. Often on long expeditionary walks in the countryside they would be joined by their favourite visitor Coleridge.

Later journals covered the siblings' travels in other parts of the Lake District, in Scotland and on the Continent, sometimes with Mary or the companionable Coleridge in the party. Some of the material in the text was recycled by William in his poetry. For so long overshadowed by her famous brother, it can now be seen that Dorothy Wordsworth was herself a writer of considerable merit, the quality of the prose, as much as the content, elevating the journals into the realms of literature.

DIARY OF A NOBODY

First published in 1892, *The Diary of a Nobody* by George and Weedon Grossmith is a comic gem. A novel in the form of a private diary, it spans fifteen months in the life of Charles Pooter. The Pooters (with wife Carrie and son Lupin) have just moved into their new house, 'The Laurels', in Holloway, a suburb of London. Pooter is a clerk in the City, a diligent husband and father, anxious to preserve an aura of social gentility and acutely sensitive to any perceived slight; of which there are many. Pooter's raison d'être for his journal comes at the start of the book: 'I have often seen reminiscences of people I have never even heard of, and I fail to see – because I do not happen to be a "Somebody" – why my diary should not be interesting.'

The Grossmith brothers were not writers by profession. George (1847–1912) was an actor and music-hall entertainer, Weedon (1854–1919) an artist. Over and above the delicious humour, their book (illustrated by Weedon) is a window onto the contemporary scene, from the décor in the Pooters' new home to the latest fad of the bicycle.

PASTORAL CARE

The diary of the Reverend Francis Kilvert, first published in the 1930s, has become a minor classic. Kilvert (1840–79) was himself the son of a clergyman. After being ordained, he served for several years as curate in the Radnorshire village of Clyro. He then returned to his father's parish near Chippenham in Wiltshire, before a final stint in Bredwardine, a small village near Hay-on-Wye in Herefordshire, where he died of peritonitis a month after his wedding.

This forms the background of the diary, which spans the years 1870–79. Kilvert's account of his activities as a country clergyman in mid-Victorian times introduces the reader to a fascinating cast of local characters. There are evocative descriptions of the landscape of Wiltshire and the Welsh borders, and of their flora and fauna. The hardships of rural life are on view along with its charm. There are some dramatic moments, including a vivid report of two innocent bystanders being beaten to death in Chippenham during a market-day brawl between men of the town and those from villages outside. What finally makes the diary so appealing however is the Reverend Kilvert himself, his innate good nature and his unsparing concern for others.

FRATERNAL COLLABORATORS

Brothers Edmond and Jules de Goncourt did everything together. They lived together, socialised together, wrote novels, historical studies and books of art criticism together, and together they created one of the most celebrated diaries in world literature. They lived in Paris, and kept a close watch on all that went on around them. Edmond (1822–96) was the more serious character, the responsible elder brother. Jules (1830–70) was livelier, with a mischievous streak. Neither married, sharing a deep-seated fear of women, though for a while they shared the same mistress.

The diary gets off to an auspicious start in December 1851, on the day their first novel is published and Louis Napoleon seizes power in a *coup d'état*. And that is how it continues, their own lives intertwined with the big events of the day. The Goncourts moved in bohemian circles as well as in high society, and the diary teems with impressions of both, cultural matters alongside spicy gossip. They survived the 1870 siege of Paris by the Prussian army and the violence of the Commune. When Jules died that same year (of syphilis, contracted twenty years earlier), the bereft Edmond closed the diary – only to reopen it a few months later, carrying on the good work alone until his own death in 1896.

STREAMS OF CONSCIOUSNESS

Virginia Woolf (1882–1941) was one of the most innovative writers of the twentieth century. A contemporary of the Irish novelist James Joyce, she too experimented with narrative techniques such as 'stream of consciousness' (in which a character's thoughts and feelings are presented in a continuous and seemingly unstructured flow) in her fiction. With her husband, the political theorist and author Leonard Woolf, she was one of the leading lights of the so-called 'Bloomsbury Group', an influential ensemble of English writers, artists and intellectuals. Her modernist novels include *Mrs Dalloway* (1925), *To the Lighthouse* (1927) and *The Waves* (1931). She also wrote several seminal feminist works, the best known of which is *A Room of One's Own*, published in 1929.

Between 1915 and 1941, Virginia Woolf kept a diary, totalling some thirty manuscript journals (later published in five printed volumes). In this she not only recorded the quotidian details of her life but also examined her approach to the art of writing and the creative process in general, with some shrewd and not always friendly comments about her fellow scribes. She wrote of her lifetime struggle with mental illness and of her series of nervous breakdowns. The final entry in her diary was written the day before she filled her pockets with stones and drowned herself in the River Ouse, near her home in Sussex.

UNEARTHING ADRIAN MOLE

The eponymous teenager made his first appearance in *The Secret Diary of Adrian Mole, Aged 13 ¾* (1982). Adrian's fictional daily reckoning of his life hilariously addresses the typical preoccupations of adolescence, set against the backdrop of the Thatcher years. Like his creator Sue Townsend (1946–2014), Adrian was born in Leicester, though the family later moves to the more posh-sounding Ashby-de-la-Zouch. The son of working-class parents, he has an indifferent academic record at school and a girlfriend named Pandora. Following the success of the first book, Townsend went on to write seven more, Adrian progressing from his teens into adulthood. In the last volume, *Adrian Mole: The Prostrate Years* (2009), the diarist has reached the age of 39 ¼, both his marriage and prostate in trouble.

EROTIC ADVENTURES

Born in Paris to Cuban parents, Anaïs Nin (1903–77) maintained a journal for some sixty years of her life, starting at the tender age of eleven. She began work as an artist's model and married her first husband, a banker and sometime experimental filmmaker, when she was twenty. Undergoing psychoanalysis in 1932 liberated her; so much so that she had affairs with both her psychiatrists. From then on, as explicitly related in her diaries, she had a string of lovers, including a lustful affair with the American writer Henry Miller (and possibly with his wife June too). She became the first woman of any note to pen female erotica and to write freely about women's sexuality.

In 1939, with war approaching, Nin and her husband Hugh (who requested not to be mentioned in her diary, given all the other men in her life) moved to the USA. In New York she met the man who would become her second husband – an ex-actor named Rupert Pole, sixteen years her junior. Without relinquishing her first husband, Nin bigamously set up home with Rupert in California, while continuing to act as Hugh's wife in New York (Hugh knew nothing about his opposite number until after his wife's death). The sexually agile Nin described her shuttle between the two men as her 'bicoastal trapeze'.

IT'S A FACT!

In May 1967, the playwright Joe Orton (whose theatre hits include *Entertaining Mr Sloane* and *Loot*) wrote in his diary: 'To be young, good-looking, healthy, famous, comparatively rich and happy is surely going against nature.' Three months later his long-time companion Kenneth Halliwell killed him in a fit of jealous rage.

POLITICAL REVELATIONS

Conservative politician Alan Clark (1928–99) was the son of Kenneth Clark, the well-known art historian. Alan rose to the rank of junior minister under Margaret Thatcher, and wrote several books on military history including *The Donkeys* (1961), a study of the Western Front in 1915. Clark, a flamboyant character, walked the corridors of power with an insouciant air. Never destined for the highest office, he nevertheless conveyed a sense of entitlement that marked him out from more run-of-the-mill politicians. An impression that was reinforced with the publication of his diaries, the first volume of which covered the years 1983–92 and caused a sensation.

Clark's outspoken comments about his colleagues in the House of Commons and in government raised a few eyebrows. But not as many as the frank revelations about his sexual peccadilloes, which most notably included an all-embracing affair with the wife of a South African judge and her two daughters. Clark cheerfully referred to the trio as 'the coven'. Two further volumes of the diary were published (a prequel and a sequel) featuring other colourful episodes from his professional and private lives.

BIKERS' MANIFESTO

In January 1952, Alberto Granado, a 29-year-old Argentinian biochemist, and his 23-year-old compatriot Ernesto Guevara, a medical student, set off from Buenos Aires on a motorcycle journey across South America. Their principal means of transport was a single-cylinder 1939 Norton 500cc, which they christened *La Poderosa* (The Mighty One). The nine-month expedition took in Argentina, Chile, Ecuador, Peru, Colombia, Venezuela, Panama and Miami. They climbed the Andes, floated down the Amazon and trekked across the Atacama Desert. In all, they clocked up over 8,000 kilometres.

The two men saw with their own eyes the poverty, degradation and exploitation of the South American people: the brutal suppression of political freedoms, the social injustice meted out to mineworkers and others, the cruel ostracism of lepers. The experience made a lasting impression on them both, and Ernesto in particular vowed to do something about it. Better known as 'Che' Guevara (1928–67), he devoted the rest of his life to fomenting Marxist revolution across the continent. First published in English in 2003 – the original Cuban edition predating it by eleven years – *The Motorcycle Diaries* (*Diarios de Motocicleta*) became a bestseller, and later a film.

THIRTY-SOMETHING

The extent to which *Bridget Jones's Diary*, published in 1996, struck a chord is reflected in the book's mammoth sales and subsequent hit movie. Created by Helen Fielding (1958–), originally for her column in the *Independent* newspaper, the thirty-something Bridget, a single woman living in London, is hilariously worried about her weight, her over-indulgence in alcohol and cigarettes, her career prospects, and most of all her single status, binging on self-help books and recording her anxieties and activities in her diary. A bestselling sequel, *Bridget Jones: The Edge of Reason*, was published in 1999, followed fourteen years later by *Bridget Jones: Mad About the Boy* (two further films have kept abreast of the books) – a story likely to be continued.

BY ROYAL APPOINTMENT

Ben Jonson was the first English poet to receive a royal pension, a grant from James I in 1616. Others followed but it was not until 1668 that the first Poet Laureate was officially appointed, Charles II bestowing the honour on John Dryden (1631–1700), the most eminent literary figure of his time. In the 350 years since then, Dryden has had just nineteen successors.

The longest-serving of them was Alfred, Lord Tennyson (1809–92), who held the post for forty-two years. Following his death in 1892, the position was kept vacant for three years as a mark of respect. Robert Southey (Laureate 1813–43), William Wordsworth (1843–50), John Betjeman (1972–84) and Ted Hughes (1984–98) are among the distinguished poets to have fulfilled the role. Not all the appointees, however, have commanded universal esteem. Of Colley Cibber, a minor eighteenth-century versifier who was twenty-seven years in the job, fellow poet Alexander Pope wrote:

> *Cibber! write all thy Verses upon Glasses,*
> *The only way to save 'em from our Arses.*

William Wordsworth's appointment in 1843 upset some of his followers, dismayed that he was joining the literary establishment. Robert Browning dashed out a poem entitled 'The Lost Leader' which began: 'Just for a handful of silver he left us / Just for a riband to stick in his coat.' He needn't have worried; Wordsworth composed no state-sponsored verse during his seven-year tenure.

Poet Laureate is an appointment for life, although not all have served that long. The incumbent is expected (though not obliged) to commemorate in verse important national events and, in more recent times, to promote the advancement of poetry within the community. In 2009, Carol Ann Duffy was inducted as Britain's first female – and first Scottish – Poet Laureate.

GRIM REAPINGS

Writers have made some bizarre exits from life, in scenarios that would stretch even *their* imaginations. The essayist Francis Bacon (1561–1626) died of pneumonia, having caught a chill whilst stuffing a fowl with snow to preserve it. The lyrical German poet Rainer Maria Rilke (1875–1926) was a fatal victim of blood poisoning after being cut by the thorn of a rose he had plucked for a young female companion. Having taken a swig of Parisian tap water to prove it was safe to drink, English man of letters Arnold Bennett (1867–1931) contracted typhoid and died (as he lay dying in his Baker Street apartment, the local authority laid straw on the road to deaden the traffic noise).

IT'S A FACT!

The poet Percy Bysshe Shelley drowned on 8 July 1822, at the age of twenty-nine, when his boat (the *Don Juan*) went down during a sudden squall in the Gulf of Spezia, off the coast of Italy. It was ten days before the body was washed ashore, identifiable only by

Shelley's clothes and by the volume of John Keats' poems he had in his pocket.

PISTOLS AT DAWN

Next to the tsar, the author Alexander Pushkin (1799–1837) was the most celebrated man in Russia. Poet, playwright, novelist, and short story writer, Pushkin was a literary one-man band. His family pedigree was suitably exotic. He was descended on his father's side from an ancient noble family. His mother's grandfather, Abram Gannibal (Russian for Hannibal), was a native of Abyssinia and godson of Peter the Great. As a young man, Pushkin led a wild life, gambling and womanising. His political views aroused the suspicions of the authorities and for a time he was exiled from his beloved St Petersburg. But the creative juices never ceased to flow. His most famous work is *Eugene Onegin* (1831), a novel in verse, which later, like his short story 'The Queen of Spades', was turned into an opera by Tchaikovsky.

In 1831, Pushkin married the eighteen-year-old Natalya Goncharova; but the writer soon became irritated by his young wife's frivolous social life. One man in particular paid court to her: Baron Georges d'Anthès. When the jealous Pushkin received an anonymous letter informing him that he had been elected to 'The Most Serene Order of Cuckolds', he challenged d'Anthès to a duel. On 25 January 1837, on the outskirts of St Petersburg, the two men faced each other in the snow. Pushkin was mortally wounded and died two days later.

IT'S A FACT!

Following his death in Germany in 1904, the body of the great Russian writer Anton Chekhov was returned to Moscow in a refrigerated railway wagon used for transporting oysters.

COFFEE BREAK

Honoré de Balzac (1799–1850) might be characterised as a French Charles Dickens; his countrymen would put it the other way round, perhaps, but either way, he is one of the world's greatest novelists. His first success, *Les Chouans*, about peasants who supported the royalist cause during the French Revolution, was published when Balzac was thirty. Over the next twenty years he wrote more than ninety novels and stories under the umbrella title of *La Comédie Humaine* ('The Human Comedy'). Balzac created a vast canvas of contemporary French life, portraying people of every social class and profession. Together, the books reflect the manners and morals of an entire society. The pages teem with more than 2,000 characters, some of them cropping up in several novels.

Balzac himself was a short, stocky man of superhuman energy, motoring on just four hours' sleep a night. He was constantly in debt, hiding from creditors in a secret room in his house. He had countless mistresses (a matter not altogether unconnected from his money problems), marrying one of them five months before he died. To help fuel his phenomenal work ethic, Balzac drank up to forty cups of coffee a day, an estimated 50,000 in his lifetime. No surprise then that the cause of death has been put down to caffeine poisoning.

MARVELLOUS BOY

The sixteen-year-old Thomas Chatterton (1752–70) from Bristol nearly pulled off one of the most remarkable literary forgeries of all time after he composed a number of poems in an archaic style of his own invention, and passed them off as the work of a non-existent fifteenth-century monk named Thomas Rowley. He sent the poems to Horace Walpole, at the time one of the country's most distinguished writers, who declared they were genuine. Chatterton promptly uprooted to London, hoping to make his own career as a poet, but almost immediately the Rowley verses were denounced as a fraud – not least by Thomas Gray, famous for his 'Elegy Written in a Country Churchyard' (1751). Finding himself penniless and starving, his hopes dashed, Chatterton declined his landlady's charitable offer of a meal and took to his room with a bottle of arsenic. He was found dead the next morning. His collected poems were published thirty-three years after his death, and William Wordsworth paid tribute to him in his poem 'Resolution and Independence' (1807): 'I thought of Chatterton, the marvellous Boy…'

J'ACCUSE!

In September 1902, the eminent French novelist Émile Zola (1840–1902) was found dead in his bedroom at his Paris home. His wife, Alexandrine, was unconscious in her own room. Both, the investigating magistrate swiftly decided, had been victims of carbon-monoxide poisoning. But friends of Zola were convinced it was murder, the writer having made many enemies over his public intervention in the Dreyfus Affair.

Captain Alfred Dreyfus, a Jewish officer in the French army, had been sent to Devil's Island for life, convicted of betraying military secrets to Austria. To liberal intellectuals in French society it was apparent that Dreyfus was a victim of anti-Semitism and a scapegoat of reactionary right-wing forces within the military and government. Zola wrote a 4,500-word open letter to the president of France, published in the newspaper *L'Aurore* on 13 January 1898. The headline read: '*J'Accuse…!*'

Following the publication of the letter, Zola was sued for libel and fled to England. He returned to France a year later but received several death threats. Meanwhile, growing public support for Dreyfus had resulted in a new trial which saw the falsely accused officer freed (he was finally exonerated and reinstated in the army in 1906). A former stove-fitter confessed on his deathbed to having killed the writer twenty-five years after Zola's demise. He alleged that as an 'anti-Dreyfusard', working on the roof next door to the Zola home, he had deliberately blocked their chimney with malicious intent.

IT'S A FACT!

In the 1950s, two of the twentieth century's foremost literary intellectuals, Arthur Koestler (1905–83) and Albert Camus (1913–60), drunkenly raced each other on all fours across the Place Saint-Michel in Paris's Latin Quarter.

MAN OF CONSCIENCE

Erskine Childers (1870–1922) was born in London, but following the early death of his parents he was sent with his siblings to live at the family home in Ireland. He read law at

Cambridge and planned a career in politics. A staunch supporter of the British Empire, he saw service in South Africa during the Boer War. Sailing became a passion and he made frequent sea-going sorties across the Channel. His experiences afloat inspired his novel *The Riddle in the Sands* (1903) – a prescient tale about a German plot to invade Britain – which enjoyed huge popularity at the time. During the First World War, Childers worked in naval intelligence and won the Distinguished Service Cross. However, he grew increasingly concerned about the on-going troubles in Ireland and was sympathetic to the republican cause.

He moved to Dublin in 1919 with his American wife Molly. Now fully committed to Irish republicanism, he took on a series of high-profile roles. When civil war broke out between the republicans and nationalists, Childers became a marked man. He was arrested and tried at a military tribunal for possessing a semi-automatic pistol, a gift from the late republican leader Michael Collins. Found guilty, he was sentenced to death by firing squad. His final words to his executioners were: 'Take a step or two forward, lads, it will be easier that way.' His son Erskine Hamilton Childers served as fourth president of the Irish Republic fifty years later.

RITUAL KILLING

Yukio Mishima is the nom de plume of Kimitake Hiraoka (1925–70), novelist, poet, playwright, actor and film director. He adopted the pseudonym to spare his father, a civil servant, the professional embarrassment of having an author for a son. Regarded as one of Japan's foremost writers of the twentieth century, his best-known novels include *Confessions of a Mask* (1949) – a semi-autobiographical work about a young homosexual – and *The Sea of Fertility* tetralogy (1969–71).

Mishima was an ardent nationalist, obsessed with the cult of the samurai. He formed his own militia group, the *Tatenokai* (Shield Society), dedicated to preserving traditional Japanese values and the glorification of the emperor.

In November 1970, Mishima and four armed cohorts inveigled their way into a Tokyo military base and captured the commandant. Mishima then tried to persuade the soldiers at the camp to stage a *coup d'état* and restore the emperor to power. When they laughed at him, he took the honourable way out by falling on his sword. The final act of the suicide ritual was decapitation, but the man assigned the task did a botched job and it took several attempts to detach Mishima's head from the rest of him. Some cynics have suggested that the true motivation for the writer's suicide was the winning of the 1968 Nobel Prize by his fellow novelist Yasunari Kawabata.

IT'S A FACT!

Margaret Mitchell (1900–49), author of the American Civil War saga *Gone With the Wind* (1936), died after being struck by a speeding vehicle in her home town of Atlanta. The governor of Georgia ordered the flag over the State Capitol to be lowered to half-mast until after her funeral.

POLITICALLY INCLINED

Over and above the mass of undistinguished memoirs, a number of politicians have made their mark in literature. The most outstanding of them is Winston Churchill (pen name Winston S. Churchill), winner of the 1953 Nobel Prize in Literature. Despite a lengthy career at the centre of politics, not least his wartime years at the helm, Churchill (1874–1965) was the author of around forty books including a four-volume biography of his illustrious ancestor John Churchill, *Marlborough: His Life and Times* (1933–38); a six-volume account of *The Second World War* (1948–53); a four-volume *History of the English-Speaking Peoples* (1956–58); and, on a lighter note, an historical adventure novel, *Savrola*, published in 1900.

Another literary occupant of 10 Downing Street was Benjamin Disraeli (1804–81), author of several popular novels. For his last book, *Endymion* (1880), Disraeli was paid £10,000 upfront, the highest publishing advance of the nineteenth century. Queen Victoria's favourite prime minister, he once quipped: 'When I want to read a novel, I write one.' It is a line that might have been said by Jeffrey Archer (1940–), whose chequered political career has been eclipsed by his success as a bestselling writer of fiction with global sales in excess of 330 million copies, and still rising.

Former senior Cabinet ministers Michael Foot (1913–2010) and Roy Jenkins (1920–2003) were both distinguished biographers. Foot's subjects included his political hero Aneurin Bevan and the writer H. G. Wells. Jenkins wrote highly acclaimed lives of Winston Churchill and William Gladstone. Another politician-turned-biographer is William Hague (1961–) who has produced books about William Pitt the Younger, and the nineteenth-century reformer William Wilberforce. Douglas Hurd (1930–), ex-foreign secretary, is the author of several political thrillers as well as a number of non-fiction titles. The veteran politician Roy Hattersely (1932–) has written fiction, biography and popular history, as well as 'ghosting' his dog Buster's diary. And then there is Boris Johnson (1964–), journalist-turned-politician and a literary jack-of-all-trades.

Some writers have tried to become politicians. In 1990, the Nobel Prize-winning author Mario Vargas Llosa (1936–) unsuccessfully ran for the presidency of Peru. The American novelist, playwright and essayist Gore Vidal (1925–2010) twice failed to make it onto Capitol Hill. One man who did succeed in his political ambition was the Czech playwright and former dissident Václav Havel (1936–2011), who became his country's president after the fall of the Soviet Union.

Which just leaves Benito Mussolini (1883–1945). In 1909, before he came to power, the Italian dictator wrote a bodice-ripping novel entitled *The Cardinal's Mistress*, which was eventually published in 1928. It was Mussolini's sole venture into fiction – unless, that is, you count his political speeches.

THE OTHER
WINSTON CHURCHILL

Winston Churchill (1871–1947) was a popular American writer of historical fiction at the turn of the twentieth century. His second novel, *Richard Carvel* (1899), sold around two million copies and was followed by several other bestsellers over the next decade.

Having become a wealthy man, Churchill abandoned his writing career in 1919 and, like his more famous namesake, took up painting. The two Churchills, who were unrelated, actually met and occasionally communicated. They agreed that, to avoid any confusion, the British version should publish under the name Winston Spencer Churchill. This was later shortened to Winston S. Churchill.

OTHER PEOPLE'S LIVES

‘*A well-written life is almost as rare as a well-spent one.*’

THOMAS CARLYLE (1795–1881)

Our appetite for reading about the lives of other people shows no sign of diminishing. In the biography section of bookshops serious studies of literary and historical figures jostle for space with more ephemeral accounts of pop-culture celebrities. It all began a long time ago.

NOBLE GREEKS AND ROMANS

The Roman biographer and historian Suetonius (AD *c.*69–*c.*122) was private secretary to the emperor Hadrian, which gave him an inside track on how things operated at the highest level. The work for which he is principally remembered is *De Vita Caesarum* (commonly known as *The Twelve Caesars*), a lively account of the life and times of the first dozen emperors of the Roman Empire, starting with Julius Caesar. It is thanks to Suetonius that we know the omnipotent Julius suffered from epilepsy.

Another biographer was at work round about the same time: Plutarch (AD c.46–120). Born in Chaeronea, Greece, Plutarch served for many years as a priest at the temple of Apollo at Delphi. It is known that he travelled to Athens and Rome, but information about his personal life remains sketchy (sadly neither he nor Suetonius had biographers of their own). *Parallel Lives* (also called *Plutarch's Lives*) is his great legacy. A work of impressive ambition, it sets out to compare the lives of famous Greeks and Romans, illustrating their strengths and weaknesses, their vices and virtues. His subjects are treated in pairs, one Greek, one Roman (for example, Alexander the Great is juxtaposed with Julius Caesar) in order to make direct comparisons. In its surviving state, the book comprises twenty-three such pairings plus four single profiles. Plutarch's *Parallel Lives* is an informative and entertaining exercise in biography, though not always historically accurate. Shakespeare drew heavily on the book for his plays *Julius Caesar*, *Coriolanus* and *Antony and Cleopatra*.

IT'S A FACT!

Dr Samuel Johnson (the doctorate was honorary) was known as the 'Great Cham of Literature', a sobriquet bestowed on him by fellow writer Tobias Smollett (1721–71). The word 'Cham', now obsolete, is synonymous with 'Khan', as in the ruler of the Tartars and Mongols, and was intended to reflect Johnson's pre-eminence within the literary establishment. It is not to be confused with 'sham', which would have meant something far less complimentary.

BRIEF LIVES

Antiquarian and biographer John Aubrey (1626–97) has two claims to fame. A keen archaeologist, he discovered the Neolithic site at Avebury in Wiltshire (the county of his birth), which boasts the largest stone circle in Europe. And his book *Brief Lives*, a collection of short profiles of some of his famous contemporaries (or near contemporaries), is an outstanding early example of the biographer's art.

Aubrey's colourful pen portraits are a blend of gossipy anecdotes and first-hand observations, with a few historical facts thrown in. His subjects include dramatists William Shakespeare and Ben Jonson, scientist Robert Boyle (of 'Boyle's Law' fame), alchemist and astrologer John Dee, astronomer Edmond Halley (who gave his name to the comet), explorer and adventurer Sir Walter Raleigh, and the philosopher Thomas Hobbes – who, we are told, first met Aubrey when the biographer was eight years old.

LOCKED-IN LIFE

The French journalist Jean-Dominique Bauby (1952–97), editor-in-chief of *Elle* magazine, was forty-three when he suffered a massive stroke. Mentally aware but paralysed from the neck down, a condition known as locked-in syndrome, Bauby embarked on the most challenging autobiographical project ever. His only means of communication was blinking his left eye; but by the use of an ingenious code, the stricken writer was able to respond to individual letters of the alphabet and spell out words. Ten months and 200,000 blinks later *The Diving Bell and the Butterfly* was finished.

In the book, the author unsparingly describes his locked-in existence and recalls life before his stroke. The 'diving bell' represents his trapped condition; the 'butterfly' the freedom of his mind. Jean-Dominique Bauby died in 1997, two days after the publication of his astonishing book.

BRINGING THE DOCTOR TO LIFE

The 16th of May, 1763, is a red-letter day for students of biography. It is the day on which James Boswell (1740–95) first met Dr Samuel Johnson (1709–84), an event which prefaced the greatest biographical work in the English language. The two men came face to face in Davies's Bookshop in London's Covent Garden. The 22-year-old Boswell was overawed at meeting the august man of letters. He apologised for being Scottish, adding: 'I cannot help it.' To which Johnson tartly replied: 'That, Sir, I find, is what a very great many of your countrymen cannot help.' Boswell recorded his first impressions of the good doctor: 'A Man of a most dreadful appearance. He is very slovenly in his dress and speaks with a most uncouth voice. Yet his great knowledge, and strength of expression command vast respect and render him excellent company. But his dogmatical roughness of manners is disagreeable. I shall mark what I remember of his conversation.'

And that is precisely what Boswell did, on and off, for the next twenty-one years. He would occasionally jot down something during a conversation, but generally relied on his prodigious memory to record the day's events and verbal exchanges, writing them up in his voluminous journal each night. He returned to Scotland to practise law and travelled extensively in Europe (meeting two other giants of the age, the French philosophers Voltaire and Jean-Jacques Rousseau) but visited London periodically to renew his relationship with Johnson. In 1773, the pair made a celebrated tour of Scotland and the Hebrides, an account of which was published twelve years later.

Boswell had informed Johnson of his intention to write a biography in 1772, but it wasn't until after his friend's death that the project got underway. The author's legal training came in handy as he waded through the minutiae of the great man's life. *The Life of Samuel Johnson, LL.D* finally made its appearance in 1791, to be greeted by popular and critical acclaim. It has been that way ever since.

BIOGRAPHERS' LIVES

Three of Britain's most distinguished biographers have a literary partner in their life. Claire Tomalin (1933–), whose biographical subjects include Jane Austen, Samuel Pepys, Thomas Hardy and Charles Dickens (as well as his mistress Nelly Ternan), is married to the novelist and playwright Michael Frayn. Michael Holroyd (1935–), the author of books about Lytton Strachey, Augustus John and George Bernard Shaw, is the husband of novelist Margaret Drabble. Richard Holmes (1945–), best known for his literary lives of the poets Shelley and Coleridge, is the long-time partner of novelist Rose Tremain.

EMINENT BIOGRAPHER

Lytton Strachey (1880–1932) was a prominent member of the Bloomsbury Group and practised to the hilt its tolerant approach to personal relationships; for the last sixteen years of his life he lived in a *menage à trois* with the painter Dora Carrington and her husband Ralph Partridge. He first achieved fame as a writer with *Eminent Victorians*, published in 1918. The book consists of four lengthy biographical profiles of the eminent Victorians in the title: Cardinal Manning, Florence Nightingale, Dr Thomas Arnold (the reforming headmaster of Rugby School) and General Gordon (of Khartoum). Strachey's serious but less than reverential portraits of these Victorian icons heralded a new biographical style, combining psychological insight with urbane wit. His full-length biography *Queen Victoria*, which followed three years later, carried on in the same vein and proved even more successful with the reading public. Just how 'amused' Queen Victoria would have been by her biographer's own lifestyle is anybody's guess.

IT'S A FACT!

Despite a scandalously varied sex life that involved affairs with men, women and her stepson, the writer Colette (1873–1954), author of *Gigi* (1945), was the first Frenchwoman to receive a state funeral. The French novelist and writer, who seductively wrote about the pains and pleasures of love, was also the first woman to report from the battlefront during the First World War.

PHONEY TITLE

The Autobiography of Alice B. Toklas (1933) is not what it says on the packet. The book is, in fact, the autobiography of the American writer Gertrude Stein, but written as though the author were her long-time partner Alice. Between the wars, Gertrude Stein (1874–1946) was an expatriate living in Paris. A poet, novelist, critic and art collector, she was an influential figure in the modernist movement (the often misquoted line 'Rose is a rose is a rose is a rose' is from her 1913 poem 'Sacred Emily'). Her home at 27, rue de Fleurus, which she shared with Alice B. Toklas (1877–1967), became a meeting place for some of the century's cultural icons. James Joyce, Ernest Hemingway, F. Scott Fitzgerald and Ezra Pound were among the literary talents who would drop in for a chat. Pablo Picasso, Henri Matisse and the cubist painter Georges Braque represented the visual arts. As Alice herself put it: 'The geniuses came and talked to Gertrude Stein and the wives sat with me.'

The book, when it came out, didn't please everybody. Hemingway, a protégé of Stein, ungraciously dismissed it as a 'damned pitiful book', and Matisse was annoyed by the way his wife Amélie had been portrayed. As for the eponymous Alice, she was just content to take the credit.

JUST BEING CATTY

Kitty Kelley (1942–), whose car sported the personalised number plate MEOW, has made a handsome living revealing home truths about the rich and famous. In a series of sensational unauthorised biographies, she has delved into the lives of Jackie Onassis, Nancy Reagan, Frank Sinatra, the British Royal Family and Oprah Winfrey, among others, lifting the lid on secrets her subjects would much prefer to have kept hidden. Kelley had a taste of her own medicine when a less-than-flattering biography about her, *Poison Pen* by George Carpozi, appeared in 1991. But Kitty's claws are still out.

LAID BARE

The gay liberation movement had barely begun when the distinctly liberated Quentin Crisp published his revealing memoir, *The Naked Civil Servant* (1968). At a time when homosexuality was still a criminal offence in the UK, and society itself aggressively homophobic, Crisp courageously flaunted his sexual preferences. Born Denis Charles Pratt (1908–99) in Surrey, Crisp's change of name was part of a makeover that included dying his hair lavender, applying nail polish to his fingers and toes, and wearing androgynous clothing. He worked as an artist's model in art education establishments (employed as such by the Department of Education he was technically a civil servant, albeit one who spent his working hours in the nude – hence the title of his book) and for a while was a male prostitute. Rejected for military service during the Second World War, he took to befriending lonely American servicemen on the home front.

Despite its explicit content (or perhaps because of it), *The Naked Civil Servant* achieved only modest sales when first published. That is until the 1975 TV dramatisation of the book, and a brilliant performance by John Hurt in the title role, changed all that. On the back of the book's subsequent success,

Quentin Crisp became a gay icon with his own one-man show in America. He was still in outrageous mode when he died aged ninety-one.

FINAL CHAPTER

Paris's three great cemeteries are the stuff of literary pilgrimage. At Père-Lachaise are the tombs of Honoré de Balzac (1799–1850), Colette (1873–1954), Molière (1622–73), Marcel Proust (1871–1922), Gertrude Stein (1874–1946), Oscar Wilde (1854–1900) and Richard Wright (1908–60). Interred at Montmartre are Alexandre Dumas fils (1824–95), Edmond de Goncourt (1822–96), Heinrich Heine (1797–1856) and Stendahl (1788–1842). While at Montparnasse can be found Charles Baudelaire (1821–67), Simone de Beauvoir (1908–86), Samuel Beckett (1906–89), Guy de Maupassant (1850–93), Eugène Ionesco (1909–94), George Sand (1804–76) and Jean-Paul Sartre (1905–80).

Entombed in the Panthéon, majestically located in the capital's Latin Quarter and the final resting place of some of France's greatest citizens, are the mortal remains of Voltaire (1694–1788), Jean-Jacques Rousseau (1712–78), Alexandre Dumas père (1802–70), Victor Hugo (1802–85) and Émile Zola (1840–1902).

TEN CLASSIC MEMOIRS

Goodbye to All That (1929)
Robert Graves

Testament of Youth (1933)
Vera Brittain

Down and Out in Paris and London (1933)
George Orwell

My Family and Other Animals (1956)
Gerald Durrell

A Moveable Feast (1964)
Ernest Hemingway

The Autobiography of Malcolm X (1965)
Malcolm X/Alex Haley

I Know Why the Caged Bird Sings (1969)
Maya Angelou

Long Walk to Freedom (1994)
Nelson Mandela

Angela's Ashes (1996)
Frank McCourt

The Year of Magical Thinking (2005)
Joan Didion

THE SPYING GAME

*'The greatest advantage of being a writer is
that you can spy on people.'*
GRAHAM GREENE (1904-91)

There has always been an affinity between the intelligence services and the literary world. During the First World War, several famous writers were recruited into MI5 and the Secret Intelligent Service (SIS), later to become known as MI6. Some of those experiences found their way into books.

Sir Compton Mackenzie (1883–1972), the author of bestselling novels including *Sinister Street* (1914) and *Whisky Galore* (1947), was engaged in clandestine activities which only came to light in 1932 on the publication of his book *Greek Memories*, describing his SIS involvement in the Eastern Mediterranean. The writer was convicted at the Old Bailey of breaching the Official Secrets Act. He was fined £100 and the book was suppressed.

W. Somerset Maugham (1874–1965), novelist, dramatist and one of the most popular short story writers of all time, converted his SIS experiences into *Ashenden: Or the British Agent* (1928): a collection of short stories featuring the title character, a playwright recruited by British Intelligence during The Great War. Ashenden is finally despatched on a mission to Russia – it is 1917 – to help keep the country's provisional government (the tsar having been deposed) on track in the war against Germany. Maugham himself had been sent on a similar assignment, getting out of Russia just before the Bolsheviks took control.

MARRYING INTO THE BOLSHEVIKS

Arthur Ransome (1884–1967), author of the Swallows and Amazons series of children's books, was one of the few Western journalists to witness the 1917 Russian Revolution at first hand. Not only did he report on it but he openly applauded it, causing many in Whitehall to label him a Bolshevik. SIS, with no one else to fall back on, took the more pragmatic step of making him an agent, code name S76. But even his new spymasters could not have anticipated Ransome's next move, which was to marry Evgenia Shelepina, private secretary to Leon Trotsky, one of the leaders of the revolution. The Ransomes settled for a while in Estonia, with Arthur making regular visits to Moscow in his role as a journalist. The couple finally returned to England in 1924 and settled in the Lake District, where Ransome, a keen fisherman, swapped political revolution for the calmer waters of Swallows and Amazons.

SPYING IN GREENELAND

Graham Greene was SIS's most famous literary recruit during the Second World War. The author had a pedigree in this line of work. His uncle Sir Graham Greene had helped set up Naval Intelligence in the earlier world conflict (another uncle, Herbert, had less admirably leaked naval information to the Japanese round about the same time) and his sister Elisabeth was secretary to the head of the SIS Middle Eastern section. After the normal vetting and training procedures, Greene was sent to Freetown in Sierra Leone, next door to the Vichy-controlled colony of French Guinea. The author drew on his experiences in Freetown for his 1948 novel *The Heart of the Matter*.

Greene's boss in counter-intelligence was Kim Philby, later to be exposed as the most infamous of Soviet spies. The two men were to remain friends for many years, leading some to believe that Greene himself might have been a double agent. In fact, Greene continued to carry out assignments for the SIS after his official release from the organisation in 1944, his status as an internationally known writer providing useful cover for visiting trouble spots such as Vietnam and Cuba. His experiences in the cloak-and-dagger world were fed into such novels as *The Quiet American* (1955), set in French Indo-China (later Vietnam), the black comedy *Our Man in Havana* (1958) and *The Human Factor* (1978), in whose central character there are echoes of Kim Philby.

IT'S A FACT!

At the age of eight, Allen Dulles, head of the CIA from 1953 to 1961, wrote a history of the Boer War. The 31-page book, first published in 1902, is still in print.

CODE NAME 17F

Ian Fleming joined Naval Intelligence in 1939 as assistant to the head of the service, rising to the rank of commander on a par with his fictional alter ego James Bond, and was code-named 17F. Like Bond, the eloquent and charismatic Fleming was a womaniser and a heavy drinker and smoker. He was said to have been the author of the so-called Trout Memo, which proposed that espionage warfare against the Germans should be conducted along the lines of fly fishing: using bait to lure the unsuspecting enemy into a situation in which they could be attacked. Fleming also played a key part in Operation Mincemeat, an imaginative plan which involved planting a corpse with documents indicating that the Allies were going to make a landing in Crete in 1943, rather than in Sicily, the actual destination. The ruse worked, wrong footing the Germans and arguably saving thousands of Allied lives.

One project of which he was solely in charge was Operation Goldeneye, the blueprint for a spy network in Spain to be activated in the event of a Nazi takeover in the country. Fleming was demobbed in 1945 and joined the Kemsley newspaper group whose flagship publication was *The Sunday Times*. In 1952, the day after his marriage to Ann Charteris, with whom he had had a long affair (he was her third husband), the former naval intelligence officer began work on *Casino Royale* (1953), launching 007's spectacular career on Her Majesty's secret service. Goldeneye was the name he gave to his Jamaican home, where he was to write all seventeen of the Bond novels.

IT'S A FACT!

President John Kennedy was a great fan of the Bond novels and listed *From Russia with Love* (1957) among his ten favourite books, an endorsement that caused sales of the novel to soar in the USA.

SOVIET AGENT

Ernest Hemingway (1899–1961) inspired a generation of young writers with his muscular narratives and ground-breaking style, to which his own macho way of life gave a glamorous authority. In the First World War he had served as an ambulance driver on the Italian Front, an experience that provided the setting for what many believe to be his finest novel, *A Farewell to Arms* (1929). In 1937, he went to Spain to report on the Spanish Civil War. Fiercely anti-fascist, Hemingway supported the Republican cause and mixed with guerrilla fighters and elements within the Communist-led International Brigades, gleaning background material for another celebrated novel, *For Whom the Bell Tolls* (1940). Round about this time he met a representative of the NKVD (the forerunner of the KGB), who recruited him – according to their files – as a Soviet agent. He was given the code name 'Argo', after the ship in which Jason and the Argonauts sailed in Greek mythology.

There is little evidence that Hemingway fulfilled any particular function in his new role, beyond promoting the anti-fascist message to the American people. He was invited to Moscow, but before he could take up the offer Pearl Harbour was attacked and America itself entered the war. Now that they were on the same side, Hemingway offered his support to the US government and proposed setting up a counter-intelligence group in Havana, where he lived. In December 1942, whilst patrolling the waters off Cuba in his boat *Pilar*, the writer reported a U-boat sighting, which the US Navy followed up. However, the writer's most famous moment of the war came twenty months later when he personally 'liberated' the bar at the Hôtel Ritz in Paris, during the battle to free the city. At the time the Germans were busy elsewhere, but it made a great story.

MAN ON THE SPOT

The thriller writer Frederick Forsythe (1938–), author of *The Day of the Jackal* (1971), *The Odessa File* (1972) and *The Fourth Protocol* (1984), worked unofficially for MI6 for twenty years. He was first approached during the Biafran War in Nigeria, which he was covering as a journalist. His intelligence gathering for that led to other assignments in Rhodesia and South Africa. Later he was sent to East Germany (still behind the Iron Curtain) to collect a package from an MI6 asset there, the rendezvous taking place in a public toilet.

UNDER THE COVERS MISSION

Young readers of *Charlie and the Chocolate Factory* (1964) and *The BFG* (1982) might be excited to learn that the creator of the stories was once a British agent, though the exact nature of some of his activities might best be left until the children have grown up. Roald Dahl (1916–90) had been a fighter pilot during the Second World War, seeing action in East Africa, Greece and Egypt. On one occasion he was forced to crash land, fracturing his skull, splintering his nose and temporarily losing his sight. He eventually returned to the sky, flying many more missions before the knock-on effects of his injuries caused him to be invalided back to Britain. Unfit to resume combat duties, in 1942 Dahl was posted to the British Embassy in Washington as assistant air attaché.

A war hero and in uniform, Dahl cut a dashing figure in the US capital. Wealthy female socialites queued up for his intimate attentions, and the young flight lieutenant seldom disappointed them. One was Claire Booth Luce, an influential congresswoman and wife of Henry Luce, owner of *Time* magazine. The Canadian spymaster William Stephenson recruited Dahl for his espionage operation linked to MI6, and the resourceful and well-connected new agent was able to pass on some useful intelligence about the Washington establishment, including insider information about President Roosevelt himself. No doubt he also cultivated a few ideas for the stories to come.

IN FROM THE COLD

David Cornwell, better known as John le Carré (1931–), had a miserable childhood. His mother left the family home for another man when David was five, and his father was a serial fraudster who lived extravagantly on his not inconsiderable wits and charm and on other people's money. David was privately educated at Sherborne, a well-known school in Dorset, but left prematurely at sixteen to study German at the University of Bern in Switzerland. It was there that he was first approached by someone in the British intelligence service, who asked him to keep an informal eye on left-wing activities amongst the students. When, later, he enrolled at Oxford University he was recruited by MI5 to infiltrate the Communist students group.

After a spell teaching at a preparatory school in Somerset and at Eton, David applied to join MI5 and was taken on at the London headquarters. The pay was poor and much of the work routine. The sister service MI6, with its counter-intelligence role, offered a more exciting prospect and, in 1960, David made the switch. Following training in espionage techniques, he was posted to Bonn, then the West German capital and a hotbed of spies. He ran agents in the field. Still strapped for money, and now with a wife and young family to support, John le Carré (as he chose to call himself) wrote his first novel, *Call for the Dead* (1961), the text of which had to be vetted by his employers. The book was a critical success, but it was his third novel that proved the career-changer. *The Spy Who Came in from the Cold* (1963) was a financial blockbuster and No. 1 on the *New York Times* bestseller list for thirty-five weeks. David Cornwell resigned from the intelligence service in 1964 – the former spy would never again feel the cold.

IT'S A FACT!

A talented artist as well as writer, John le Carré (as 'David Cornwell') illustrated two wildlife books – *Talking Birds* (1961) and *Animals and Ourselves* (1962) – by a former MI5 colleague, Maxwell Knight.

WATERGATE AUTHOR

In the early hours of the morning on 17 June 1972, five men were arrested for attempted burglary and wiretapping at the Democratic National Committee headquarters in Washington. It was the beginning of the so-called Watergate scandal that was to bring down President Richard Nixon. One of the two men who organised the break-in was E. Howard Hunt (1918–2007), a part-time consultant at the White House. Hunt was a former CIA operative, a veteran of the 1961 Bay of Pigs fiasco – the botched attempt to overthrow Cuban dictator Fidel Castro. He had been engaged in a number of shady activities for the Nixon administration before his career hit the buffers over Watergate. Three months after the original arrests, Hunt and his co-conspirator G. Gordon Liddy were charged with the crime. Both men served time in prison, Hunt's sentence eventually reduced to a little under three years.

In addition to his covert intelligence work, Hunt had a productive sideline as a writer of thrillers and spy novels – *Bimini Run* (1949), *The Violent Ones* (1950), *Return from Vorkuta* (1968) and *The Gaza Intercept* (1981), to name but a few. Some of the books were written under his own name, others were published pseudonymously; as befits a man used to working undercover. Hunt also wrote several volumes of memoirs, the last and most revealing of which – *American Spy: My Secret History in the CIA, Watergate and Beyond* – was published after his death in 2007.

IT'S A FACT!

Len Deighton's (1929–) spy thrillers *The Ipcress File* (1962), *Funeral in Berlin* (1964) and *Billion Dollar Brain* (1966) are narrated by the same anonymous character. In the film versions of the books the character is given the name 'Harry Palmer', and as played by Michael Caine became one of the most celebrated screen spies in cinema history.

FEMME FATALE

No one knows if Moura Budberg (1892–1974) was really a spy or not, but she certainly had all the right connections. Born in Ukraine, she was married to a tsarist diplomat, Count Johann von Benckendorff, but had embarked on a series of affairs before her husband (with whom she had two children) was murdered by a peasant in 1919. One passionate relationship was with the British agent Robert Bruce Lockhart, who was in Russia ostensibly as his country's first envoy to the new Bolshevik regime. Both he and Moura were arrested as suspects following an assassination attempt on Lenin, although they were not implicated. Lockhart was freed as part of a prisoner exchange; Moura took the short cut of seducing her interrogator.

Her next notable conquest was the Russian writer Maxim Gorky (1868–1936) whose secretary and common-law wife she became (his legal wife lived in another part of the house with her own lover). When Gorky left Russia to live in Italy, Moura followed him, stopping off in Estonia for a year to marry another aristocrat, whom she promptly divorced though she kept the title. Homesick for Mother Russia after eight years abroad, Gorky headed back to his native land without Moura. But in 1936, as he lay dying, she returned to say farewell, sharing the moment with Joseph Stalin and the notorious head of the secret police, General Yagoda.

It was at Gorky's home years earlier that she had met the author H. G. Wells (1866–1946), and he became her next serious lover. Although she declined to marry him, they remained close until his death. During the Second World War she worked for the British Ministry of Information, mixing with government ministers and a host of other important people. In the 1950s, the Soviet spy Guy Burgess (before his cover was blown) was a regular visitor to her London home. Many were convinced Moura was a Russian agent; others thought she worked for British Intelligence. Neither party claimed ownership.

IT'S A FACT!

Moura Budberg was the great aunt of Britain's former deputy prime minister, Nick Clegg.

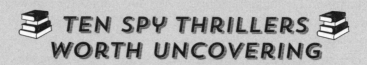

TEN SPY THRILLERS WORTH UNCOVERING

The Riddle in the Sands (1903)
Erskine Childers

The Secret Agent (1907)
Joseph Conrad

The Thirty-Nine Steps (1915)
John Buchan

Epitaph for a Spy (1938)
Eric Ambler

The Spy Who Came in from the Cold (1963)
John le Carré

The Human Factor (1978)
Graham Greene

Berlin Game (1983)
Len Deighton

Kingdom of Shadows (2000)
Alan Furst

The Company (2002)
Robert Littell

Slow Horses (2010)
Mick Herron

WORLDS OF IMAGINATION

One of the literary perks of writers of fiction is that they can create and populate their own worlds. Not all of them take up the option, of course. Many authors find enough room to manoeuvre within existing territorial and social boundaries. But others colonise their own imagination: as with Narnia, the fantasy world created by C. S. Lewis (1898–1963), accessed through the prosaic portal of a wardrobe; or Anthony Trollope's (1815–82) earnestly provincial Barsetshire, the county setting for six of his best-known novels.

WESSEX TALES

Most of the major novels and short stories of Thomas Hardy (1840–1928) are located in his native Dorset – or 'Wessex', as the author chose to call it. Wessex had been the Anglo-Saxon kingdom of Alfred the Great prior to the Norman Conquest, and the name had lain dormant for centuries. Hardy, the son of a village stonemason, appropriated the ancient title for his fictional world, which stretched into the adjacent counties of Devon, Wiltshire and Hampshire. The first reference to Wessex comes in Hardy's fourth published novel, *Far from the Madding Crowd* (1874). This was followed by other 'Wessex' novels such as *The Return of the Native* (1878), *The Mayor of Casterbridge* (1886), *The Woodlanders* (1887) and *Tess of the d'Urbervilles* (1891).

In the fictional Wessex, names of towns and villages are changed (though some natural features and ancient monuments like Stonehenge retain their real identity). The county town of Dorchester becomes Casterbridge; Shaftesbury is Shaston; Weymouth is turned into Budmouth Regis, and Bournemouth is Sandbourne. Among the many villages rebranded is Hardy's birthplace of Upper (now 'Higher') Bockhampton, which is called Upper Mellstock in the novels. After his death it was decided that the final resting-place of Hardy, who was equally renowned as a poet, should be in Poets' Corner at Westminster Abbey. The writer himself, however, had opted for the parish church at Stinsford (a.k.a 'Mellstock'), near to where he was born. It called for a very British compromise. Hardy's ashes, minus his heart, were ceremoniously interred in the Abbey, where they could be duly honoured by the nation. His heart was then buried separately in Dorset – where it had always been.

YOKNAPATAWPHA COUNTY

William Faulkner (1897–1962) wrote: 'I discovered my own little postage stamp of native soil was worth writing about and that I would never live long enough to exhaust it.' He called this 'postage stamp' Yoknapatawpha County (the Chicasaw Indian word for 'furrowed ground'; they being the first inhabitants of the region). According to the author, the invented county comprises 2,400 square miles, with a population of 15,611 – 6,298 whites and 9,313 blacks.

Born in Mississippi, Faulkner spent a brief period in Paris after the First World War before returning to his native state, where he wrote practically all of his novels and short stories, including masterpieces such as *The Sound and the Fury* (1929), *As I Lay Dying* (1930), *Light in August* (1932) and *Absalom, Absalom!* (1936), which explore the social, racial and sexual tensions in the aftermath of the American Civil War. The whole spectrum of a decaying Southern society is encompassed in the fictional world of Yoknapatawpha County ('William Faulkner, sole owner & proprietor'). By the end of the 1930s Faulkner's work was out of print and he himself was largely forgotten, but a post-war resurrection saw the writer awarded the Nobel Prize in 1949, cementing his place as one of the giants of American literature.

HOBBIT LAND

'In a hole in the ground there lived a hobbit.' So begins what became one of the best-known English stories of the twentieth century: *The Hobbit*, published in 1937, by the South African-born J. R. R. Tolkien (1892–1973), son of British parents and professor of Anglo-Saxon (Old English) at Oxford University. Tolkien's follow-up book was *The Silmarillion*, but his publisher turned down an early draft (it was finally published posthumously in 1977) and requested instead a sequel to the Hobbit tale. In 1955, sixteen years later, the first book in *The Lord of the Rings* trilogy appeared. Although it received mixed reviews from the critics (predictably his friend C. S. Lewis, a fellow academic, was one of those who praised it), the work quickly acquired a huge following amongst the reading public, developing into a cult that would be re-energised half a century later by a series of blockbusting movies.

The stories take place in 'Middle-earth', which broadly represents the Old World of the planet Earth (named Arda in the books) in a fictional pre-historic era. Middle-earth is lived in and fought over by an enormous cast of elves, dwarves, humans, dragons, warrior orcs, trolls, wizards, tree-like ents, and of course hobbits – among others. Each has its own language and history, combining to create a fantasy world of compelling complexity. Sales to date of *The Hobbit* alone comfortably top 100 million copies. Not bad for a vertically challenged, middle-aged, hairy-footed creature with a name like Bilbo Baggins.

LAKE WOBEGON

Garrison Keillor (1942–) unveiled Lake Wobegon in 1974 on the Saturday night radio programme, *A Prairie Home Companion*, which he created and went on to host for over forty years. In the segment called 'News from Lake Wobegon', he told stories about the inhabitants of the imaginary place ('somewhere in the middle of the state, but not on the map'). These light-hearted, personalised tales became the most popular feature on the show and attracted a listening audience way beyond the Minnesota state lines. His first book on the subject, *Lake Wobegon Days* (1985), was an immediate bestseller, introducing to an eager reading public the mythical Minnesota town 'that time forgot, that the decades cannot improve'.

Keillor added characters as the radio tales and then the printed stories and novels evolved. The action, as unhurried as Keillor's laconic delivery, moves back and forth in time, embracing humour, sadness and romance. Much of the humour flows from the interaction between the German immigrant families, who are mainly Catholic, and their Lutheran fellow citizens of Scandinavian descent. It all adds up to a nostalgically affectionate portrait of small-town America 'where all the women are strong, all the men are good-looking, and all the children are above-average'. It doesn't get more mythical than that.

IT'S A FACT!

The American writer Edgar Rice Burroughs (1875–1950), creator of Tarzan, added another string to his literary bow with a series of action-adventure stories set in a fantasy realm called Pellucidar, an inner world 500 miles beneath the surface of the earth. In one crossover story, Tarzan the ape-man hangs out there.

DISCWORLD

Terry Pratchett's (1948–2015) fantasy creation Discworld consists of a flat disc perched on the backs of four elephants, which themselves stand on the back of a giant turtle called Great A'Tuin. Just in case anyone should think that this bizarre structure is in any way compact, we are told that the disc is roughly 10,000 miles wide, with four continents and an encircling waterfall that pitches the world's oceans into space. Discworld has its own geographical and physical features (not to mention social ones), a multiplicity of languages, its own calendar, and magic as its principal source of energy. It is populated by humans, dwarfs, elves, fauns, gnomes, goblins, golems, gorgons, orcs, trolls and various 'undead' species such as bogeymen and zombies. There is also a ubiquitous character named Death – a seven-foot-tall skeleton in a black robe who rides a pale horse called Binky.

The first Discworld novel, *The Colour of Magic*, was published in 1983 and has been followed by forty more (the author also wrote around thirty other books). The stories engagingly send up other types of fantasy fiction and parody many aspects of real life, from religion to rock music. Even Shakespeare and Beatrix Potter come in for some genial flak. Most of all though, it is Pratchett's fabulous storytelling that accounts for Discworld's phenomenal success.

IT'S A FACT!

Samuel Butler's (1835–1902) novel *Erewhon*, published in 1872, savagely satirises the humbug and hypocrisy in Victorian society. The title is an anagram of 'nowhere'.

WHO'S REALLY WHO

'I draw from life – but I always pulp my
acquaintance before serving them up. You would
never recognise a pig in a sausage.'
FRANCES TROLLOPE (1780–1863)

Characters in novels and short stories are often based – wholly or in part – on someone known to the author, though not in most cases to the general reader. Some are a blend of several people (including perhaps the author), covering their tracks in real life. Occasionally, however, the identity of the subject is all too clear. Some of those transposed into fiction are portrayed admiringly, some maliciously; others just conveniently fit the part.

CLASSIC PROTOTYPES

The inspiration for the vivacious, comically sentimental and utterly selfish Horace Skimpole in Charles Dickens's *Bleak House* (1853) was unmistakeably, to those who knew him, the English poet and essayist Leigh Hunt (1784–1859). Dickens himself confirmed that 'the likeness is astonishing. I don't think it could be more like the man himself.' Hunt's family and friends were greatly offended by the characterisation, however close to the truth it was, so to appease them Dickens wrote a flattering profile of the poet in his magazine *All the Year Round*.

When Emily Brontë created Heathcliff, the tortured romantic hero of her novel *Wuthering Heights* (1847), it seems she had someone particular in mind. While employed as a teacher at a girls' school near Halifax in Yorkshire, the author had heard about an unpleasant local character named Jack Sharp, by then dead. Adopted as a child by a charitable uncle, the cruelly arrogant Sharp had later turned the older man out of his home and taken over his wool business. He then corrupted a younger member of the family in much the same way as Heathcliff does Hareton Earnshaw in the novel.

Long John Silver, the colourful one-legged villain in *Treasure Island* (1883) by Robert Louis Stevenson (1850–94), had an unlikely model in real life. The poet, critic and editor W. E. Henley (1849–1903) was well known in literary circles and a friend of the author. Henley's left leg had been amputated when he was in his teens to prevent the spread of a tubercular infection and as a result, according to Stevenson, he had acquired a 'maimed masterfulness', a charismatic authority which the author transferred to his fictional character. The two men later fell out, though not on Long John Silver's account.

FOUR LEGS NOT TWO

In George Orwell's allegorical novel *Animal Farm* (1945), the animals drive out the drunk and incompetent farmer Mr Jones and take over the running of the place themselves. The book is a satire on the 1917 Russian Revolution and its totalitarian aftermath. It is soon apparent that the pigs are the dominant intellectual force among the animals and two of them, Napoleon and Snowball, become the all-powerful leaders of the group. The evicted Farmer Jones can be seen as Tsar Nicholas II (though he doesn't lose his life), Napoleon is a porcine Joseph Stalin, and Snowball is Leon Trotsky, like his original eventually forced into exile. As for the rest of the animals, they end up more or less where they started.

AGENTS' DOUBLES

Richard Hannay (later Major-General Sir Richard Hannay) is the secret-agent hero of several novels by the Scottish writer John Buchan (1875–1940) – later Lord Tweedsmuir and Governor-General of Canada. The best-known Hannay adventures are *The Thirty-Nine Steps* (1915), *Greenmantle* (1916) and *Mr Standfast* (1919). During the Boer War, Buchan was private secretary to Lord Milner, High Commissioner for South Africa. It was there that he met a British intelligence officer named William Edmund Ironside, the model for his fictional leading man. The six-foot-four (1.93m) Ironside, fluent in fourteen languages, had carried out many dangerous assignments behind enemy lines. He eventually outranked Hannay, becoming Field Marshal Ironside, Chief of the Imperial General Staff at the outbreak of the Second World War.

Ian Fleming (1908–64) drew on a number of his associates in British Naval Intelligence, as well as himself, to create the legendary Commander James Bond. But the character's name is down to one man. James Bond, author of *A Field Guide to the Birds of the West Indies* (1936), was a neighbour of Fleming in Jamaica. Fleming, himself a keen bird-watcher, admired the book; and even more the ornithologist's name which, he later explained, was 'brief, unromantic, Anglo-Saxon, and yet very masculine'. Just the job for 007.

John le Carré's best known character is George Smiley, the quiet, dignified, super-effective spymaster at 'The Circus', the fictional headquarters of Britain's intelligence agency. Smiley, the antithesis of James Bond, is partly based on two individuals, both of whom played an influential role in the author's life. John Bingham, himself a writer of thrillers, was le Carré's senior officer at MI5. Among the characteristics he shared with his fictional counterpart was the habit of polishing his glasses with the end of his tie. Vivian Green taught le Carré at Oxford University and became a close friend and confidant. A man of probity and a patient listener with a profound understanding of the human condition, he had much in common with the ever-thoughtful Smiley – not least an erratic dress sense.

LOVE TRIANGLE

The Scottish author James Kennaway (1928–68), best known for his novel *Tunes of Glory* (1956), and thriller writer John le Carré were the very best of friends. Until, that is, the latter's passionate affair with Kennaway's wife Susan. The hard-living Kennaway drew heavily on the relationship between the three of them in his final novel, *Some Gorgeous Accident* (1967), published a year before his death from a heart attack. John le Carré tapped the same source for his own love triangle in *The Naïve and Sentimental Lover* (1971).

LITERARY LOOKALIKES

The title character of Virginia Woolf's novel *Orlando* (1928) was unashamedly modelled on her friend and lover Vita Sackville-West. Vita (short for Victoria) had a string of affairs with other women, among them a BBC producer, the women's editor of the *Daily Mail* and her own secretary. The poet Edith Sitwell (1887–1964) mischievously proposed her for the position of Poet Laureate, saying: 'Miss Sackville-West, had it not been for a flaw in fate, would have been one of Nature's gentlemen.'

At the outbreak of the Second World War, two of Britain's most prominent literary figures and close friends, the poet W. H. Auden (1907–73) and novelist Christopher Isherwood (1904–86) upped sticks to settle in America. Their action, construed as cowardice in some quarters, was much criticised. The writer Evelyn Waugh (1903–66) lampooned the pair in his satirical novel *Put Out More Flags*, the two émigrés thinly disguised as a couple of proletarian poets named Parsnip (Auden) and Pimpernell (Isherwood).

One of the principal characters in W. Somerset Maugham's (1874–1965) novel *Cakes and Ale* (1930) is a writer named Alroy Kear. Kear is an unflattering portrait of Sir Hugh Walpole (1884–1941), an immensely popular novelist at the time, though his books later fell out of fashion. He is best known for the *Herries Chronicle* (1930–43), a series of historical novels set in the north-west of England. The New Zealand-born Walpole was a generally likeable man and on friendly terms with Maugham. Not that that did him much good. Maugham initially denied any deliberate resemblance, but fessed up after Walpole's death. There was comeuppance of a sort after Maugham himself died in 1965. The central character in Anthony Burgess's novel *Earthly Powers* (1980), which was shortlisted for the Booker Prize, is a retired homosexual writer named Kenneth Toomey, who bears more than a passing resemblance to Maugham.

LUCKY JIM

There is something of the poet Philip Larkin (1922–85) in Jim Dixon, the eponymous hero of Kingsley Amis's comic novel *Lucky Jim* (1954). Like Jim, the jazz-loving Larkin hated 'filthy Mozart' and some of the character's inventive wordplay is reminiscent of the wittily disrespectful English poet. Amis lifted Jim's surname from Dixon Drive in Leicester, where his great friend Larkin had digs at No. 12. The book is also dedicated to Philip Larkin.

MILITARY SOURCES

Raymond Briggs's (1934–) picture book for children, *The Tin-Pot Foreign General and the Old Iron Woman* (1984), takes a pot shot at the Falklands War. Although the real conflict isn't mentioned, there is no mistaking the target: the protagonists fight over a small, insignificant island populated mainly by shepherds who eat little else but mutton. The 'Foreign General', made appropriately of tin pots, clearly represents the Argentinian dictator General Galtieri. The 'Old Iron Woman' is a warlike Margaret Thatcher – a.k.a. the Iron Lady. Only the soldiers of either side are made of flesh and blood.

You might have thought that the inspiration for the heroic rabbits Hazel and Bigwig in Richard Adams' bestselling novel *Watership Down* (1972) was a pet bunny or two. But, according to the author (1920–2016), the rabbits' prototypes were two-legged creatures, both of whom served with Adams in the airborne unit of the Royal Army Service Corps during the Second World War. Captain Paddy Kavanagh (Bigwig), a former journalist and courageous soldier, died at the Battle of Arnhem in 1944. Major John Gifford (Hazel) was the author's commanding officer and a born leader of men – and of rabbits too, as it turned out.

IT'S A FACT!

The character Norman Bates in Robert Bloch's 1959 thriller *Psycho* (later an Alfred Hitchcock film) was based on a real person. Two years before the book's publication, a Wisconsin man named Ed Gein was arrested for the murder of two women. According to the police, Gein had also been in the process of making a female outfit so that he could masquerade as his dead mother.

MODEL COINCIDENCE

The real-life models for two of the most enduring characters in children's literature – the flying ace 'Biggles' and William Brown, hero of the *Just William* stories – lived side by side without knowing of each other's fictional self. Biggles (James Bigglesworth) made his debut in book form in *The Camels Are Coming* (1932). In a career spanning some ninety-six novels and short stories, Biggles fights in both world wars, as well as having peacetime adventures in Africa, South America, Polynesia and the Caribbean. He ends up in the Special Air Police combatting crime. His creator, W. E. Johns (1893–1968), who had himself been a pilot in the Royal Flying Corps, was the prolific author of over 160 books. His model for Biggles is said to have been a former RAF officer named Cecil George Wigglesworth, who (like his fictional counterpart) rose to the rank of Air Commodore.

During the Second World War, Air Commodore Wigglesworth served in Iceland. By a bizarre twist of fate, stationed in the same RAF camp with him was John Lamburn, whose sister Richmal Crompton was the author of the *Just William* stories. Crompton had based the rascally schoolboy William Brown largely on her brother.

HOLLYWOOD CASTING

F. Scott Fitzgerald's final and unfinished novel *The Last Tycoon* (1941) was published a year after his death. Some critics believe it was potentially his finest work. The novel is set in Hollywood, where the author spent the last years of his life. Its central character, Monroe Stahr, is a movie producer and recognisably based, at least in part, on the 'boy wonder' Irving Thalberg (1899–1936), who was head of production at MGM when in his mid-twenties. Like Fitzgerald (1896–1940), Thalberg died tragically young.

Scott Fitzgerald was himself the model for a character in another critically acclaimed American novel, *The Disenchanted* by Budd Schulberg (1914–2009). The 1950 novel, which is autobiographical, is about a young screenwriter (in essence Schulberg) assigned to work on a movie with a famous author whose career has hit rock bottom. Schulberg disingenuously denied that the author (called 'Manley Halliday' in the book) was Fitzgerald, claiming it was a composite portrait of several writers. Few believed him.

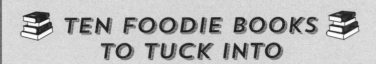

TEN FOODIE BOOKS TO TUCK INTO

French Country Cooking (1951)
Elizabeth David

The Art of Eating (1954)
M. F. K. Fisher

The New Book of Middle Eastern Food (1985)
Claudia Roden

Roast Chicken and Other Stories (1996)
Simon Hopkinson/Lindsey Bareham

The Man Who Ate Everything (1997)
Jeffrey Steingarten

How to Eat (1998)
Nigella Lawson

Kitchen Confidential (2000)
Anthony Bourdain

Thai Food (2002)
David Thompson

The River Cottage Meat Book (2004)
Hugh Fearnley-Whittingstall

The Kitchen Diaries (2007)
Nigel Slater

ASTEROIDS TO ZOMBIES

'Ever since the Industrial Revolution, science fiction has been the most important genre there is.'
IAIN BANKS (1954-2013)

Mary Shelley (1797–1851) might have been surprised to learn that her gothic fantasy *Frankenstein* (1818) would one day be widely perceived as the first great science-fiction novel. In fact, the term 'science fiction' was not coined until 1851, the year she died, and lay dormant until the 1930s. Scientific discoveries and developments throughout the seventeenth and eighteenth centuries had stimulated an interest in future civilisations and the possibility of other worlds. However, it would be some time before these speculations evolved into a literary genre. Several writers not normally associated with science fiction explored its possibilities, among them Edgar Allan Poe in his short story 'The Unparalleled Adventure of One Hans Pfaall' (1835); Sir Arthur Conan Doyle in the Professor Challenger adventure *The Lost World* (1912); and Jack London in 'The Red One' (1918), a story involving extraterrestrials.

JULES VERNE

The French writer Jules Verne (1828–1905) told good old-fashioned adventure stories with an uncanny eye to the future. In *From the Earth to the Moon* (1865), a three-manned capsule is successfully fired towards the moon by means of a gigantic space cannon. The launching pad is situated in Florida, anticipating by a hundred years the Cape Canaveral site. Captain Nemo's underwater vessel *Nautilus* in *Twenty Thousand Leagues Under the Sea* (1870) predates the world's first powered submarine by a quarter of a century. However, the most prescient of the author's novels was his first, *Paris in the Twentieth Century*, written in 1863 but not published until 131 years later.

Pitched ninety-seven years ahead, the novel is a dystopian view of a technologically advanced civilisation. Verne's publisher turned down the work on the grounds that it was too unbelievable (he didn't much rate the 'lifeless text' either), though in fact the book is full of remarkably accurate predictions. Gas-fuelled vehicles travel on asphalt roads. There are elevated and underground rail systems, electric street lights, high-rise buildings and a type of fax machine. Verne even anticipates the electric chair. The manuscript for the novel was only discovered in 1989 when a long-neglected family safe was forced open. Something that even Jules Verne wouldn't have predicted.

BURNING BOOKS

The 1953 novel *Fahrenheit 451* by Ray Bradbury (1920–2012) depicts a dystopian American society in which books are outlawed and, if discovered, burned. The title is the temperature at which paper ignites. With the book an endangered species the author anticipates the internet, describing a world overloaded with information accessed via wall-sized, flat-panelled screens. Other spot-on prognostications include ATMs, touch-activated locks and unmanned aerial drones.

H. G. WELLS

H. G. Wells (1866–1946) had a vast range as a writer, his prolific output embracing satirical and social novels (e.g. *Kipps* published in 1905 and *The History of Mr Polly* in 1910), short stories, popular works of history, science, politics and sociology. A progressive thinker, he espoused feminism, evolutionism, the advancement of science, and world government. Not all his observations have stood the test of time, but his assertion that man's scientific advances totally outdistance his intellectual and social development remains damagingly true today. His greatest literary legacy is his science fiction, and he is rightly viewed as one of the genre's most influential writers.

In a remarkable spasm of creativity, Wells produced four sci-fi classics in as many years: *The Time Machine* (1895), *The Island of Doctor Moreau* (1896), *The Invisible Man* (1897) and *The War of the Worlds* (1898), each on a different seminal theme. Much later came the prophetically titled *The Shape of Things to Come* (1933), which trailed a Second World War (Wells was only four months adrift on the start date, which in the story's case is January 1940) and accurately depicted crowded cities being destroyed by bombs from the air.

PEN FRIEND

The Canadian writer Margaret Atwood (1939–), author of several futuristic novels including *The Handmaid's Tale* (1986) and winner of the Man Booker Prize in 2000 with *The Blind Assassin*, devised a novel way of dealing with signing sessions. In 2006, the author invented a remote-controlled pen which enabled her to sign books for her fans wherever they happened to be in the world. Atwood would sign her name, along with a brief inscription, on an electronic pad while chatting to the fan on a video link from her home, or elsewhere. A couple of seconds later, at the bookshop or literary event, two metal arms holding a pen reproduced the message in the grateful recipient's book. The invention, appropriately called the LongPen, now has a wider commercial application – profitably signed off by its creator.

BIG THREE

The careers of science fiction's so-called 'Big Three' – Robert A. Heinlein (1907–88), Arthur C. Clarke (1917–2008) and Isaac Asimov (1920–92) – coincided during the latter half of the twentieth century.

ROBERT A. HEINLEIN

Robert A. Heinlein came from German-American stock that went back six generations. He grew up in Kansas City and spent several pre-war years in the US Navy before ill-health returned him to Civvy Street. He began a new career writing science-fiction stories for children, before switching to the adult genre. Among his best-known novels are the militaristic *Starship*

Troopers (1959); *Stranger in a Strange Land* (1961), whose main protagonist is a human who returns to Earth having been born on Mars and raised by Martians; and *The Moon Is a Harsh Mistress* (1966), about a lunar colony's revolt against the government on Earth. Heinlein originally espoused liberal causes but later swung politically to the ultra-conservative right, attracting accusations of fascism. He preferred to describe himself as a libertarian.

ARTHUR C. CLARKE

Somerset-born Arthur C. Clarke was a keen amateur astronomer. During the Second World War, he worked on the RAF's top-secret RADAR system and wrote stories for sci-fi magazines in his spare time. The scientific themes in Clarke's fiction (some twenty-five novels and several collections of short stories) are inventively spread far and wide, but he had a particular interest in space travel. 'The Sentinel', a short story written in 1948 for a BBC competition (it didn't even make the shortlist), was adapted twenty years later for the Stanley Kubrick film *2001: A Space Odyssey*. The film introduced Clarke to a wider audience and led to him becoming the host on a number of popular TV science programmes. In recognition of his outstanding contribution to science, an asteroid – *4923 Clarke* – was called after him. His name was also incorporated into that of a species of dinosaur unearthed in Australia, *Serendipaceratops arthurcclarkei*. He was knighted, in 2000, for his services to literature. It's a pity they couldn't have waited one more year.

ISAAC ASIMOV

Asimov's parents emigrated to the USA from Russia when he was three years old. The young Isaac grew up to become a professor of biochemistry at Boston University and a prolific writer on mainly scientific subjects. It is estimated that he wrote or edited over 500 books in his lifetime, including some of the most successful and respected science fiction ever produced. He is particularly known for two series of novels and short stories. The Foundation series (1951–93) – an epic saga on the fall and rise of galactic empires – was originally conceived as a trilogy but was later expanded through the addition of two prequels and two sequels. The Robot series (1950–1985), pitched a millennium into the future where humans have colonised fifty planets and robots (bound by the Three Laws of Robotics) are part of the scenery, is made up of five novels and thirty-eight stories. The two series overlap and some of the stories were published in magazines before appearing in book form.

CYBERPUNK

The American writer William Gibson (1948–) is credited with inventing cyberpunk, a strand of science fiction in which lawless sub-cultures exist in societies oppressively dominated by advanced technology: low life meets high tech. Gibson set the scene with his highly successful first novel *Neuromancer* (1984), set in The Sprawl, a near-future American urban environment in which everything and everyone is controlled cybernetically. It was the first in the so-called Sprawl Trilogy (1984–88). A second trilogy, The Bridge (1993–99), is located in a post-earthquake California, the abandoned Golden Gate Bridge becoming a shantytown and sanctuary for outcasts under the cosh of cybernetic control.

DUNE

Published in 1965, the novel *Dune* is considered to be the masterpiece of author Frank Herbert (1920–86). The story is set in the year 10,191 in a vast interstellar empire with individual planets ruled by noble houses that owe allegiance to the supreme emperor. One of the planets, Arrakis, is the sole source of a substance called 'melange', the most essential and valuable commodity in the universe. It is enough to set the forces of the empire at each other's throats. *Dune* is an enthralling adventure of ambition and intrigue in outer space, making some serious points about religion, politics, ecology and technology along the (Milky) way. One of the bestselling science-fiction novels ever, though it was turned down by more than a dozen publishers before making it into print, *Dune* spawned five successful sequels and a host of other media spin-offs.

UNREAL REALITIES

The science-fictional worlds of Philip K. Dick (1928–82) – the 'K' stands for Kindred – are populated by spies, aliens and robots. The nature of reality and the human (or alien) condition are underlying themes in his work, his futuristic locations generally closer to home than those of many writers in the genre. In *The Man in the High Castle* (1962), Dick's alternative history has the Axis powers as victors in the Second World War, with the USA now under the joint thumbs of Nazi Germany and Imperial Japan. The setting for *Do Androids Dream of Electric Sheep?* (1968) is the aftermath of another global conflict, this time nuclear, with a post-apocalyptic San Francisco largely destroyed along with the rest of the planet. The novel was the basis for the 1982 film *Blade Runner*. Dick, who was married five times, embraced the druggy counter-culture of the late 1950s and 1960s, an influence on his work and a contributory factor towards the severe hallucinations from which he later suffered.

IT'S AN ANDROGYNOUS WORLD

The five Earthsea fantasy novels by the American author Ursula K. Le Guin (1929–2018) have been compared to J. R. R. Tolkein's *The Lord of the Rings* and C. S. Lewis's *Chronicles of Narnia*. In her breakthrough sci-fi novel, *The Left Hand of Darkness* (1969), she creates a planet in perpetual winter with androgynous inhabitants who, except for a few fertile days each month when for sexual purposes they become male or female, have no fixed gender. The extent to which human society is shaped by sharply defined gender roles is a major theme of the book. A quirky sci-fi fact is that Ursula K. Le Guin and Philip K. Dick both graduated from Berkeley High School in California in 1947, though the two never knew each other.

MAKING A DISTINCTION

Many established science-fiction authors contribute to other literary genres. Some resent being stuck with the 'sci-fi' label; the novelist J. G. Ballard (1930–2009), most widely known for his novel *Empire of the Sun* (1984), about a young British boy's ordeal at the hands of the Japanese during the Second World War, was one such writer.

The Scottish author Iain Banks (1954–2013) found a neat way round the problem. Banks came to prominence with his debut novel *The Wasp Factory* (1984), narrated by a sixteen-year-old psychopath who lives on a remote Scottish island. This was followed by two other works of mainstream fiction. Banks then published his first science-fiction novel, *Consider Phlebas* (1987), which introduced the Culture, a galactic utopia of humanoids, aliens and artificial intelligences co-existing in an anarchic society. In order to make a distinction between this and his other fiction, the author adopted the marginally adjusted name of Iain M. Banks (the 'M' standing for Menzies). In all, he wrote twelve science-fiction novels and one short-story collection. His mainstream tally, as Iain Banks, amounts to fifteen novels and a non-fiction book about whisky.

HITCHHIKING TO SUCCESS

There aren't too many intentional laughs in science fiction, which probably explains the phenomenal success of Douglas Adams's *The Hitchhiker's Guide to the Galaxy*, which began life as a radio comedy and was first broadcast in 1978. According to the author, the basic idea came to him while he lay drunk in a field in Innsbruck, Austria – a nineteen-year-old student on a hitchhiking tour of Europe. The novel (same title) was published a year after the radio launch. Four others followed: *The Restaurant at the End of the Universe* (1980), *Life, the Universe and Everything* (1982), *So Long, and Thanks for All the Fish* (1984) and *Mostly Harmless* (1992).

The story hilariously chronicles the adventures of Englishman Arthur Dent, who is the last human to hitch a ride from Earth before the planet is destroyed to make way for an intergalactic highway. He is accompanied on his space travels by an alien named Ford Prefect, Zaphod Beeblebrox, who has two heads and three arms, a depressed android called Marvin, and Trillian – formerly Tricia McMillan, a woman Arthur once met at a party. Among other surreal delights, readers will discover that the answer to the 'ultimate question of life, the universe and everything' is – wait for it – '42'.

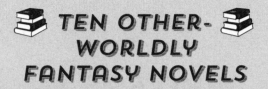

TEN OTHER-WORLDLY FANTASY NOVELS

A Wizard of Earthsea (1968)
Ursula K. Le Guin

The White Dragon (1978)
Anne McCaffrey

Parable of the Sower (1993)
Octavia E. Butler

Assassin's Apprentice (1995)
Robin Hobb

The Golden Compass (1996)
Philip Pullman

A Game of Thrones (1996)
George R. R. Martin

Gardens of the Moon (1999)
Steven Erikson

Storm Front (2000)
Jim Butcher

American Gods (2001)
Neil Gaiman

The Magicians (2009)
Lev Grossman

WRITERS IN THE DOCK

> *'All writers are thieves; theft is a necessary tool of the trade.'*
> **NINA BAWDEN (1925–2012)**

Writers have frequently been collared by the law. American author Dan Brown successfully fended off two separate legal actions for plagiarism following the publication of his blockbuster thriller *The Da Vinci Code* (2003). J. K. Rowling had a seven-year battle to clear her name, after she was accused of lifting the plot of *Harry Potter and the Goblet of Fire* (2000) from a previously published work. But sometimes the ruling has gone the other way.

WRONG ROOT

Alex Haley (1921–92) was the author of *Roots: The Saga of an American Family* (1976), which told the story of an eighteenth-century black African, Kunta Kinte, captured and sold into slavery in the USA. Though written in the form of a novel, the story allegedly stuck closely to known facts and went on to describe the lives of Kunta Kinte's descendants, the most recent of whom was Alex Haley himself: great-great-great-great grandson of KK. The bestselling book was turned into a hugely popular television series, stimulating enormous interest in the African-American heritage. Two years after the book's publication, an American writer named Harold Courlander claimed that Haley had cribbed extensively from his novel *The African* (1967). The case went to trial and was eventually settled out of court, Haley paying substantial damages. Further doubt was cast on the factual reliability of *Roots* by genealogists who challenged Haley's research into his antecedents. But by then a lot of copies had been sold.

ROGUE KNIGHT

Completed around 1470, *Le Morte d'Arthur* (*The Death of Arthur*) is the first prose version in English of the Arthurian legend, and the most famous. It was published in 1485 by the printer William Caxton (see page 13). The identity of the author is not known for certain, but the most likely candidate is Sir Thomas Malory (*c.*1415–71) of Newbold Revell in the parish of Monks Kirby, Warwickshire, who served as a soldier under the Earl of Warwick and was later elected to Parliament. Somewhere along the way he picked up a knighthood.

In 1451, it seems, things began to go wrong. Malory was accused of extorting money (presumably with menace, given that he probably carried a sword or dagger) from two fellow inhabitants of Monks Kirby. He was also charged with robbery and rape – though in those days the latter could extend to consensual sex with a married woman (by someone other than her husband, that is). Other alleged crimes, including the theft of horses, followed and Malory was briefly imprisoned, before managing to escape. Thereafter, he appears to have been in and out of prison on a regular basis, his last stint in jail – in 1468 – the result of his involvement in a plot to overthrow King Edward IV. He died near Newgate Prison in London, his last known address.

BOUNCING BACK

Joan Henry (1914–2000) was an English novelist and playwright with family connections. A former debutante, she was descended from no less than two British prime ministers: Robert Peel (1788–1850) and Lord John Russell (1792–1878), who was her great-great grandfather. The philosopher Bertrand Russell was a second cousin. After a failed marriage, she fell into debt through gambling and in 1951 was found guilty at the Old Bailey of passing fraudulent cheques and sentenced to twelve months in prison, serving eight. Her exposé of prison conditions, *Who Lie in Gaol* (1952), became a bestseller. A novel, *Yield to the Night* (1954), about a woman awaiting execution, followed and became a successful film starring Diana Dors in the central role (Henry married the film's director, J. Lee Thompson). The author went on to write several plays with judicial themes for stage and television.

LOVERS' TIFF

Paul Verlaine (1844–96) and Arthur Rimbaud (1854–91) were two of the most celebrated French poets of the nineteenth century. They met in 1871 when Verlaine was twenty-seven and Rimbaud seventeen. Verlaine was unhappily married (though his put-upon wife had more substantial grounds for discontent) and Rimbaud was a grubby teenager with some seriously unattractive social habits, albeit accompanied by poetic flair. The two men formed a romantic attachment and took off for Brussels and then London.

Their love affair was not without danger. Both men drank heavily (often imbibing the deadly absinthe) and frequently fought, sometimes with knives wrapped in towels. One such drunken spat ended with Verlaine slapping Rimbaud in the face with a wet fish. He then dramatically returned to Brussels, leaving the younger man to fend for himself in London. Not for long, however. Rimbaud caught up with Verlaine and, in what proved to be their final tiff, the latter shot him in the arm with a gun he had intended to use on himself. Verlaine was jailed for two years. Thereafter the two men followed separate paths. Rimbaud travelled widely, to the Far East and North Africa, had a leg amputated and died aged thirty-seven. Verlaine descended into alcoholism, drug addiction and poverty, dying five years after his erstwhile companion. The enduring legacy of both men is their poetry. (In a footnote to their affair, Verlaine's gun was sold at auction in 2016 for €434,500.)

BEATING THE RAP

The leaders of the 1950s American beat movement had several brushes with the law. Jack Kerouac (1922–69) was born in Massachusetts, the son of French-Canadian parents. His semi-autobiographical, trans-America, drug-fuelled novel *On the Road* (1957) provided a 'high' for a generation at odds with an affluent post-war society. In 1944, Kerouac was arrested (along with fellow writer William S. Burroughs) as a material witness in a New York waterfront murder. After the crime both men had helped the murderer, a mutual friend named Lucien Carr, dispose of incriminating evidence. Burroughs's father posted bail for his son, but Kerouac's declined to do so. The parents of Edie Parker, Kerouac's girlfriend at the time, agreed to bail him out on condition he marry their daughter. The prisoner happily obliged, the two case detectives serving as witnesses. The marriage was to last barely four years.

The poet Gregory Corso (1930–2001) was another leading light of the beat generation. At sixteen, he was sentenced to three years in Clinton State Prison, New York, for theft. It was his third jail sentence. It was while incarcerated that he began to write poetry and to read widely from the classics on the shelves in the prison library. His cell had been previously occupied by legendary Mafia boss 'Lucky' Luciano, and other mafiosi offered the vulnerable youngster protection whilst behind bars. After his release, Corso met fellow poet Allen Ginsberg (1926–97), who introduced him to other 'Beats'.

Ginsberg himself narrowly escaped jail. In 1949, he was arrested for storing in his apartment some loot stolen by friends. A prison sentence was on the cards. But a successful plea of 'psychological disability' by his lawyer resulted instead in the poet spending eight months in a mental institution.

CIVIL DISOBEDIENCE

The American essayist and poet Henry David Thoreau (1817–62) was an advocate of self-sufficiency. In 1845, he built a cabin at Walden Pond, near his home in Concord, Massachusetts, on land owned by his good friend and fellow writer Ralph Waldo Emerson (1803–82). Thoreau lived self-sufficiently (though he took his laundry home for his mother to do) in the cabin for two years, two months and two days, recounting his experiences in his most famous book, *Walden; or, Life in the Woods* (1854). On 23 July 1846, as a protest against America's war with Mexico, Thoreau refused to pay his poll tax. He was put in the Concord jail overnight but released the following morning when someone paid up on his behalf. His subsequent essay 'Civil Disobedience' was a great influence on Gandhi and Dr Martin Luther King, Jr. among others.

DANGEROUS GAME

William Seward Burroughs II (1914–97) met Joan Vollmer, nine years his junior, in New York in 1945. They were both friends of the writers Jack Kerouac and Allen Ginsberg. Burroughs, who would go on to write *Naked Lunch* (1959), was a drug addict. So too was Vollmer, who despite Burroughs's homosexuality became his common-law wife. In 1950, the couple moved to Mexico City. One night a year later they drunkenly decided to re-enact 'William Tell', with Burroughs attempting to shoot a highball glass off the top of Vollmer's head. The writer had been fascinated by guns since childhood and always carried a pistol with him. His aim clouded by alcohol, Burroughs fired too low and Vollmer was killed almost immediately. He was arrested and spent thirteen days in prison before being granted bail, at which point he skipped the country. Haunted by his wife's death, Burroughs moved restlessly around the world, his most productive writing years ahead of him. He later came to the 'appalling conclusion that I would never have become a writer but for Joan's death'.

POETIC LICENCE

François Villon, born in Paris in 1431 (the year Joan of Arc was burned at the stake) was one of France's greatest lyric poets. A brilliant student at the Sorbonne university in Paris, he gained a master's degree in the arts before he was twenty-one. Like many students, before and since, Villon indulged in some wild behaviour when away from his studies. He mixed in undesirable company. In 1455, he was involved in a violent quarrel between some of his drinking companions and a priest. In the ensuing scuffle, daggers were drawn and the priest was fatally stabbed by Villon. He was banished from Paris, only to receive a royal pardon a year later.

If this was meant to signal a change in the poet's behaviour, it didn't work. Villon was almost immediately implicated in the theft of 500 gold crowns from the College of Navarre in Paris. Again, he was forced to flee the city. In *Le Petit Testament* (1456), written when he was on the run, Villon facetiously composes his own will, bequeathing a number of worthless items to friends and enemies. This was later followed by *Le Grand Testament* (1461), an altogether more serious assessment of his life, comprising over 2,000 lines and considered Villon's masterpiece.

In 1462, and back in Paris, the poet was involved in yet another fatal street fight. This time he was condemned to death. While under sentence he wrote one of his best-known poems, 'Ballade des pendus' ('The Ballad of the Hanged Men'), in which he imagines his own demise at the end of the rope. It was to remain a figment of his imagination. Villon's sentence was commuted to a ten-year banishment. The great criminal poet left the scene, the final stanza of his life unrecorded.

FRENCH INSIDER

Although known mainly for his poetry (he wrote nearly 3,000 poems in all) and his experimentation with form and language, E. E. Cummings' (1894–1962) first published work was a novel – *The Enormous Room* (1922) – based on his internment in a French military prison during the First World War. The poet had joined the ambulance service in France and in letters home, read by military censors, he expressed anti-war sentiments. In 1917, he was arrested by the French authorities on suspicion of espionage and spent close to four months in prison. The experience didn't lessen Cummings' affection for France, the writer returning to Paris several times in later years.

SUPPLY AND DEMAND

'So many books, so little time.'
FRANK ZAPPA (1940-93)

The eighteenth-century writer-printer-bookseller Samuel Richardson would barely recognise the publishing industry of today, despite the end product being essentially the same (though he would no doubt be gratified to see that some of his own books are still in print). Galloping advances in technology have seen the printed book – from the utilitarian paperback to three-dimensional pop-ups – joined by the audiobook and eBook. Gone are the days of galley proofs and cumbersome artwork: a book's content now whizzes electronically from writer and designer to publisher and printer.

Print on demand (POD), a digital printing technology that enables small quantities of a book to be inexpensively produced on an 'as needed' basis, is changing the dynamics of publishing. Not having to print a substantial quantity upfront, and reducing the attendant problems of storage and distribution, has made it much easier for authors to publish their own work. Readers, too, have a far more active role. No longer dependent on the views of literary critics, they can post their own review comments (and read what other book buyers think) as blogs or on Amazon and Goodreads – the latter, launched in 2007, has so far catalogued over two billion titles with sixty-eight million reviews. Reading groups meet face to face or online to pick over the latest publications or to revisit old favourites.

IT'S A FACT!

According to a report by the International Publishers Association (IPA), the UK publishes more books per capita than any other country. The annual output of just under 200,000 new and revised titles is roughly four times the figure of forty years ago, and works out at around twenty new books per hour.

DOING IT YOURSELF

Self-publishing is nothing new. The English writer and clergyman Laurence Sterne (1713–68) self-published the first two volumes of his great comic novel *The Life and Opinion of Tristram Shandy, Gentleman* (1759). Unable to find a publisher for her novels, Jane Austen was forced to do likewise with three of the four books published in her lifetime. The nineteenth-century American poets Emily Dickinson and Walt Whitman, and the French novelist Marcel Proust, were among other famous writers who paid to see their work in print.

Amazon's Kindle Direct Publishing (KDP) system enables authors to upload their creative outpourings free of charge, bypassing traditional publishers and the retail network. However, since in most cases there is no professional editorial input, the standard of many of these eBooks is, at best, questionable. Nevertheless, self-publishing is here to stay, giving many deserving authors a chance to be read. And if the phenomenal success of self-published writers like E. L. James (*Fifty Shades of Grey*), Michael J. Sullivan (*The Riyria Revelations*) and Amanda Hocking (*Switched)* – who had a fistful of novels rejected before uploading her first digital fiction in 2010 – is anything to go by, there is plenty of money to be made as well.

OWN LABEL

In 1917, Virginia Woolf and her husband Leonard Woolf (1880–1969) set up a small publishing imprint at their home in Richmond, Surrey, calling it the Hogarth Press after the name of the house. Among the hand-printed volumes they produced (on a press that cost them £19) were several novels by Virginia Woolf herself, with cover illustrations by her sister Vanessa Bell. The Hogarth Press also published stories by Katharine Mansfield (1888–1923), the first UK edition of T. S. Eliot's poem *The Waste Land* (1923) and *The Edwardians* (1930), a bestselling novel by the writer and landscape gardener Vita Sackville-West (1892–1962), with whom Virginia Woolf had a decade-long affair.

IT'S A FACT!

The American writer Edna Ferber (1887–1968) was so disgusted with her first novel, *Dawn O'Hara* (1911), that she threw the manuscript in the fire. Her mother rescued it from the flames and sent it to a publisher, who promptly agreed to publish it.

FIGHTING FOR INDEPENDENCE

Fierce competition from online outlets has forced independent booksellers to become more resourceful, offering their customers an experience that cannot be matched by the internet giants. Some have a busy programme of promotional activities, embracing signing sessions, poetry readings, themed book weeks, storytelling sessions for children, and talks by authors on anything from cooking to space travel. Others broaden their appeal by selling designer stationery, posters and prints, or arts and crafts items alongside books. Many bookshops have a cafe attached (the London Review Bookshop in Bloomsbury, an offshoot of the *London Review of Books,* even has its own cake shop), adding a cappuccino or cup of lapsang souchong to the pleasures of book browsing. Sometimes the premises themselves are part of the attraction: a converted chapel, a former railway station, a canal barge. It all helps to sell books.

IT'S A FACT!

London's oldest bookshop is Hatchards in Piccadilly. Founded in 1797, it received a royal warrant from King George III and boasts the current monarch as an account customer.

SHAKESPEARE & CO

Sylvia Beach's bookshop in Paris, Shakespeare & Co, was a rendezvous for writers between the two world wars. An American ex-pat, Beach (1887–1962) spent most of her adult life in the French capital, remaining in the city throughout the Nazi occupation. She opened her English-language bookshop in the Saint-Germain-des-Prés quarter in 1919, changing premises two years later (not to be confused with the current 'Shakespeare and Company' bookstore on the Left Bank, named in honour of the original in 1964). Among the many famous ex-pat writers who gathered there was James Joyce, unable to find a publisher for his novel *Ulysses* which had been widely rejected on the grounds of obscenity and profanity. Sylvia Beach offered to publish the book herself and produced an edition of 1,000 copies. Now acknowledged as one of the greatest fictional works of the twentieth century, *Ulysses* was modestly launched on 2 February 1922 – Joyce's fortieth birthday. Less cause for celebration was the fact that the book contained some 2,000 printing errors, making the author's masterpiece even more challenging to read.

MAKING HAY

Literary festivals are a part of Britain's cultural landscape (see Resources, page 237) with the Hay Festival, first staged in 1988, the granddaddy of them all. Hay-on-Wye is a small town in Breconshire, on the Welsh border, with a resident population of around 1,500. On the face of it an unlikely venue for a literary festival, but the annual ten-day event attracts upwards of 250,000 visitors – along with many authors, wheeled out by their publishers to sign books or to subject themselves to an on-stage interview in front of a generally admiring audience. Two former US presidents have attended – Bill Clinton in 2001 and Jimmy Carter seven years later – Clinton describing the bookfest as the 'Woodstock of the mind'. A parallel festival for children – HAYDAYS – has writing workshops and other activities, and its own glitterati line-up of authors and illustrators.

There are as many as thirty bookshops in Hay-on-Wye, the least expensive of them the Honesty Bookshop, where everything sells for £1 or less, and there is no till: customers leave what they owe in the honesty box. The first second-hand bookshop opened in 1962, in what was then nothing more than a village. About fifteen years later its entrepreneurial proprietor Richard Booth, the man credited with transforming the place into a bibliophile's heaven, pronounced Hay-on-Wye an independent kingdom and himself its king. His subjects have much to thank him for.

IT'S A FACT!

In 2014, the American author Orrin Woodward set a world record for the most books signed at a single session. In the course of six hours and thirty-three minutes, he signed 6,786 copies of his book *And Justice for All*.

📚 TEN GOOD 📚 READS ABOUT THE BOOK TRADE

Shakespeare and Company (1959)
Sylvia Beach

84 Charing Cross Road (1970)
Helene Hanff

A Boy at the Hogarth Press (1972)
Richard Kennedy

Books, Baguettes and Bedbugs (2006)
Jeremy Mercer

Weird Things Customers Say in Bookshops (2012)
Jen Campbell

Bookshops (2013)
Jorge Carrión

The Bookshop That Floated Away (2014)
Sarah Henshaw

The Bookshop Book (2014)
Jen Campbell

Off the Shelf (2016)
Carol Ann Duffy

The Diary of a Bookseller (2017)
Shaun Bythell

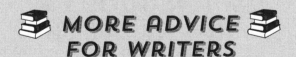

MORE ADVICE FOR WRITERS

'When people tell you something's wrong or doesn't work for them, they are almost always right. When they tell you exactly what they think is wrong and how to fix it, they are almost always wrong.'
Neil Gaiman (1960–)

'*If you want to be true to life, start lying about it.*'
John Fowles (1926–2005)

'*You can't wait for inspiration. You have to go after it with a club.*'
Jack London (1876–1916)

'*If you get stuck, get away from your desk… don't just stick there scowling at the problem.*'
Hilary Mantel (1952–)

'*Writing is a wholetime job: no professional writer can afford only to write when he feels like it.*'
W. Somerset Maugham (1874–1965)

'*Never show or discuss work in progress. Never answer a critic.*'
Raymond Chandler (1888–1959)

'*The writer must be universal in sympathy and an outcast by nature: only then can he see clearly.*'
Julian Barnes (1946–)

'*All experience is good for writers – except for physical pain.*'
William Trevor (1928–2016)

'*The role of a writer is not to say what we all can say, but what we are unable to say.*'
Anaïs Nin (1903–77)

'*It's not a good idea to put your wife into a novel… not your latest wife anyway.*'
Norman Mailer (1923–2007)

'*Don't take anyone's writing advice too seriously.*'
Lev Grossman (1969–)

GLITTERING PRIZES

'The Booker is murder. Absolutely nothing would be lost if it withered away and died.'

V. S. NAIPAUL (1932–)

Britain's two oldest annual awards are the James Tait Black Memorial Prize and the Hawthornden Prize, both dating back to 1919. The James Tait Black awards (there are three of them) are for fiction, biography and – since 2013 – drama. The Hawthornden Prize is more broadly awarded for the 'best work of imaginative literature', which can include biography, travel and history as well as fiction and poetry. The most lucrative non-fiction award, currently £30,000, is the Baillie Gifford Prize, named after the Scottish investment company that sponsors it. Previously called The Samuel Johnson Prize, it is anybody's guess what the good doctor would have made of the change in nomenclature.

Literary awards have proliferated in recent years; prestige spiced with cash prizes. For winners of the more high-profile awards a hike in sales generally accompanies the windfall. Not all authors are comfortable with the media hype that surrounds these events, but the boost to their earnings (not to mention those of their publishers and agents) is usually compensation enough.

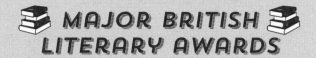

MAJOR BRITISH LITERARY AWARDS

Costa Book Awards
(five categories + Book of the Year) £60,000 (total)

Man Booker Prize (fiction) £50,000

Man Booker International Prize (translated fiction)
£50,000

David Cohen Prize (for body of work in English)
£40,000

Bailey's Women's Prize for Fiction £30,000

International Dylan Thomas Prize (best literary work
by someone under forty) £30,000

Baillie Gifford Prize (non-fiction) £30,000

William Hill Sports Book of the Year £29,000

Walter Scott Prize (best historical fiction) £25,000

Rathbone Folio Prize
(best literary work, excluding children's books)
£20,000

James Tait Black Memorial Prizes (fiction/biography/
drama) £10,000 (each)

PRIZE LEGACIES

In 1947, W. Somerset Maugham created an annual literary prize in his own name. The Somerset Maugham Award, administered by the Society of Authors, is given each year to a British writer (or writers: in recent years there have been multiple winners) under the age of thirty-five. The prize money is to be spent on travelling abroad, with a view to enriching the recipient's work (Maugham's own extensive travels are reflected in many of his novels and short stories). The 1955 award went to Kingsley Amis for his debut novel *Lucky Jim*; his son Martin was to win it nineteen years later for *his* first novel, *The Rachel Papers*. Kingsley Amis, who had an aversion to foreign travel, stayed at home and used the money to fund his next novel, appropriately titled *I Like It Here* (1958).

Betty Trask was a writer of romantic fiction about whom very little is known, though her name lives on in the form of a generous literary bequest. The Betty Trask Prize and Awards (the fund was bequeathed to the Society of Authors in 1983) go to British and Commonwealth writers under the age of thirty-five for a first novel. Unusually, the work can be unpublished. The annual pot of £20,000 is split between the Betty Trask Prize, the winner of which receives £12,000, and the Betty Trask Awards, which are for varying amounts depending on the number of recipients. To be eligible, novels must be written in a 'traditional or romantic, but not experimental, style'. Latter-day James Joyces need not apply.

PULITZER PRIZE

The American Pulitzer Prize awards embrace journalism, literature and music. There are currently twenty-one award categories, including fiction, history, biography/autobiography, general non-fiction, poetry and drama. The Hungarian-born American newspaper magnate Joseph Pulitzer (1847–1911) endowed New York's Columbia University with funds to establish a prize in his name. The first awards were made in 1917.

THE BOOKERS

The Man Booker Prize is awarded annually for the best original novel written in the English language. The Man Booker International Prize is awarded for a single work of fiction, translated into English and published in the UK. Each award is worth £50,000, though in the case of the International Prize the money is shared equally between author and translator. The shortlisted runners-up receive £2,500 apiece. Launched in 1969 as the Booker-McConnell Prize (after the original sponsors), eligible works had to be from the Commonwealth, Ireland, South Africa or (later) Zimbabwe. In 2014, this qualification was extended to any English-language novel, and two years later Paul Beatty (1962–) became the first American writer to win the award, for his novel *The Sellout*.

The first winner of the Booker, with a prize of £5,000, was P. H. Newby (1918–97) for his novel *Something to Answer For*. Newby, a broadcasting executive, later became managing director of BBC Radio. A year later Bernice Rubens (1923–2004) became the first female recipient of the prize, with *The Elected Member*. The first author to win the prize twice was South Africa's J. M. Coetzee (1940–), for *Life & Times of Michael K* (1983) and *Disgrace* (1999). The Australian writer Peter Carey

(1943–) emulated the feat with *Oscar and Lucinda* (1988) and *True History of the Kelly Gang* (2001).

Hilary Mantel (1952–) established another Booker 'first' by winning the award for each of the first two volumes of a trilogy, her ongoing historical saga about Thomas Cromwell: *Wolf Hall* (2009) and *Bring Up the Bodies* (2012).

BOOKER DRAMA

In 1972, the Marxist novelist and art critic John Berger (1926–2017) picked up the prize for his novel G. At the award ceremony, Berger criticised Booker, McConnell Ltd for historically exploiting the sugar trade in the Caribbean. He then donated half his £5,000 prize money to the British wing of the revolutionary Black Panther movement.

There was further drama in 1980 when two of the UK's foremost novelists appeared to be neck-and-neck for the prize: Anthony Burgess (1917–93) with *Earthly Powers* and William Golding (1911–93) with *Rites of Passage*. Burgess let it be known that he would only attend the ceremony if his victory was confirmed in advance. The result went down to the wire, with the judges arriving at their decision just thirty minutes before the official announcement. Golding won, but his principal competitor wasn't there to congratulate him.

Irvine Welsh's controversial novel *Trainspotting* (1993), with its violent language and graphic portrayal of drug addiction, was removed from the Booker shortlist allegedly because it offended the sensibilities of two of the judges. The book's Scottish author later observed that the award is 'based on the conceit that upper-class Englishness is the cultural yardstick against which all literature must be measured'. Having served on the judging panel in 1996, another Scottish novelist, A. L. Kennedy, broke ranks and labelled the award a 'pile of crooked nonsense'. Over the years, the judges have been variously accused of elitism and of dumbing down; and, from time to time, of making the wrong choice. It all helps to sell a lot of books.

DAGGERS DRAWN

The British Crime Writers Association introduced its annual Dagger awards in 1955, just two years after its own inception. It began with a single award, the Crossed Red Herring, renamed the Gold Dagger after five years. Today there are ten Daggers handed out, including Gold (best crime novel of the year); Diamond (for authors whose writing careers have been marked by sustained excellence); Ian Fleming Steel Dagger (best thriller novel of the year); Dagger in the Library (for authors most popular with users of public libraries) and International Dagger (best crime novel not originally in English). Collectively, the shortlisted candidates represent a who's who of modern British crime fiction – plus a few unusual suspects.

NOBEL LAUREATES

The first-ever recipient of the Nobel Prize in Literature – in 1901 – was the French poet René François Armand Sully Prudhomme (1839–1907), who probably deserved it for the length of his name alone. Six years later Rudyard Kipling (1865–1936) became the first British writer to receive the honour; aged forty-one at the time, he remains the youngest-ever recipient. Two Irishmen, the poet William Butler Yeats (1865–1939) and the playwright George Bernard Shaw (1856–1950) followed in the 1920s. It wasn't until 1930 that an American writer made it onto the list of laureates: Sinclair Lewis (1885–1951), whose best-known work includes the novels *Main Street* (1920) and *Babbitt* (1922). On four occasions, the last in 1974, the prize has been shared by two writers.

In 1953, Sir Winston Churchill became the only British prime minister to receive the award ('for his mastery of historical and biographical description as well as for brilliant oratory'). On the evidence of those who have followed him at No. 10 Downing Street, there seems little prospect that his feat will be emulated. The French writer and philosopher Jean-Paul Sartre (1905–80), who made a point of declining official honours, turned down the award when it was offered to him in 1964.

The Swedish Academy of Literature, which makes the all-important annual selection, has frequently been accused of political bias and of rewarding writers of esoteric reputation. (Hands up all those who have heard of Theodor Mommsen (who won in 1902), Verner von Heidenstam (in 1916), Grazia Deledda (in 1926), Halldór Laxness (in 1955) and Alexis Léger (a.k.a. Saint-John Perse, in 1960).) Almost as significant as those chosen are those left out in the cold – among them, Leo Tolstoy (1828–1910), Mark Twain (1835–1910), Marcel Proust (1871–1922), James Joyce (1882–1941), Vladimir Nabokov (1899–1977) and Graham Greene (1904–91).

IT'S A FACT!

Of the 109 recipients of the Nobel Prize in Literature up to 2016, only fourteen have been women. When the British writer Doris Lessing (1919–2013) won the award in 2007, she was aged eighty-eight years and fifty-two days – the oldest winner of either sex.

TEN OTHER DESERVING WRITERS WHO FAILED TO WIN THE NOBEL PRIZE

Anton Chekhov (1860–1904)
Henry James (1843–1916)
Joseph Conrad (1857–1924)
Rainer Maria Rilke (1875–1926)
Thomas Hardy (1840–1928)
Edith Wharton (1862–1937)
Virginia Woolf (1882–1941)
H. G. Wells (1866–1946)
Jorge Luis Borges (1899–1986)
Iris Murdoch (1919–99)

RUSSIA WITHOUT LOVE

The Russian poet and novelist Boris Pasternak (1890–1960) became a *cause célèbre* in the West following the publication of his novel *Doctor Zhivago*. The work had been rejected in his own country but an English version came out in 1958 to great acclaim, and in the same year Pasternak was awarded the Nobel Prize. The delighted author fired off a telegram to the Swedish Academy, saying he was 'infinitely grateful, touched, proud, surprised, overwhelmed'.

The paranoiac Soviet authorities didn't share his elation. Suspecting a Western plot, they orchestrated demonstrations against Pasternak and ran damaging editorials about him in the state-controlled press. He was informed that if he went to Sweden to collect his medal, he would not be permitted to return to the Soviet Union. Under pressure, Pasternak despatched a second telegram, this time courteously declining the prize. The Nobel Committee awarded it to him nevertheless, merely regretting that he was unable to accept it in person.

LATE PICK-UP

Another Russian recipient of the Nobel Prize to fall foul of the Soviet authorities was Alexander Solzhenitsyn (1918–2008). In 1945, the writer had been arrested for criticising the Stalin regime and served eight years in various prisons and labour camps. Released following Stalin's death in 1953, Solzhenitsyn continued his writing career with some of his works smuggled out of the country for publication overseas, including the novels *Cancer Ward* and *The First Circle*, both published in the UK in 1968.

In 1970, the author received the nod from the Nobel Committee but, like Boris Pasternak before him, was unable to leave the country for fear of not being allowed back in. Four years later, the Soviet government solved the problem for Solzhenitsyn by expelling him from the country. He belatedly collected his medal at the 1974 ceremony.

GRAND PRIX

The *Prix Goncourt,* France's most prestigious literary prize, was founded in 1903 in honour of the brothers Edmond (1822–96) and Jules (1830–70) de Goncourt, novelists and critics whose joint *Journal* is a masterly and often scurrilous record of the period (see page 114). The prize is awarded annually by the Académie Goncourt for the best new work of French fiction (four other awards have since been added: for biography, poetry, first novel and short story). The ten members of the academy debate the merits of the candidates over monthly dinners at the restaurant Drouant in Paris, their regular meeting-place since 1914. The winning author receives the symbolic sum of ten euros, but is guaranteed massive sales from the large book-buying French public. Distinguished past winners include Marcel Proust (1871–1922), André Malraux (1901–76), Simone de Beauvoir (1908–86) and Marguerite Duras (1914–96).

There have been several controversies surrounding the prize, not the least of them the case of previous winner Romain Gary (1914–80), who won for a second time in 1975 after submitting the novel *La Vie Devant Soi* (*The Life Before Us*) under the nom de plume 'Émile Ajar'. The unwritten rule being that no one should receive the prize more than once, the deception remained secret until after the author's death. Writers who miss out on *le Goncourt* can always hope to pick up one of France's other literary prizes, numbering – at the last count – over 1,150.

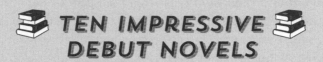

TEN IMPRESSIVE DEBUT NOVELS

Ingenious Pain (1997)
Andrew Miller

White Teeth (2000)
Zadie Smith

The Kite Runner (2003)
Khaled Hosseini

The Curious Incident of the Dog in the Night-Time (2003)
Mark Haddon

Brick Lane (2003)
Monica Ali

The Book Thief (2005)
Markus Zusak

The Brief Wondrous Life of Oscar Wao (2007)
Junot Díaz

The White Tiger (2008)
Aravind Adiga

The Tiger's Wife (2009)
Téa Obreht

The Help (2009)
Kathryn Stockett

NAMING NAMES

Many writers have resorted to a pen name: some for professional or political reasons (including keeping out of jail); others for commercial or collaborative considerations. Some pseudonyms are transgender or deliberately neutral in that respect; some a passport to a different literary genre. Some authors tentatively hide behind an alias at the start of their careers and find that it sticks. Others simply fancy another name.

IT'S A FACT!

Washington Irving (1783–1859) was America's first internationally famous author. Among his best-known short stories are 'Rip Van Winkle' (1819) and 'The Legend of Sleepy Hollow' (1820). Irving wrote under a number of extravagant pseudonyms, among them: Geoffrey Crayon, Gent., Friar Antonio Agrapida, Launcelot Langstaff, Jonathan Oldstyle and Diedrich Knickerbocker.

WHAT'S IN A NAME?

Mathematician and logician Charles Lutwidge Dodgson (1832–98), creator of *Alice's Adventures in Wonderland* (1865) and of her follow-up experiences *Through the Looking-Glass* (1872), enjoyed puzzles and word games. So when it came to finding a suitable pseudonym under which to publish his far-from-logical fantasies, he took a predictably convoluted route. Translated into Latin, 'Charles Lutwidge' becomes *Carolus Ludovicus* – an anglicised version of which is 'Carroll Lewis'. Reverse this (as if you were seeing it through a looking glass) and you arrive at Lewis Carroll.

Charles Dickens's pen name 'Boz', under which he published many of his earlier writings (collected as *Sketches by Boz*, 1836–7), had a more mundane origin. His baby brother Augustus was nicknamed 'Moses' after a character in Oliver Goldsmith's *The Vicar of Wakefield* (1766), a favourite family book. When spoken with a blocked nose, the result of head colds that ricocheted around the Dickens household, this sounded like 'Bozes', and hence 'Boz'.

Eric Arthur Blair (1903–50) was teaching at a small private school in England when his first book was accepted for publication. The author felt in need of a pseudonym and put forward a number of names to his publisher Victor Gollancz, one of which was 'H. Lewis Allways'. Gollancz opted for the less pretentious 'George Orwell' (named after the Suffolk river which the writer knew well), *Down and Out in Paris and London* was published in 1933, and the rest is literary history.

Not all pen names can be traced so precisely. Over the years David Cornwell, alias John le Carré, has come up with various explanations of how he arrived at his; none of them apparently true. But then, as a former spy, he is used to covering his tracks.

British writer Derek Lindsay (1920–2000) published just one novel, and even that wasn't under his own name. Critical praise was heaped on *The Rack* when it appeared in 1958. The author A. E. Ellis (Lindsay's pseudonym) was compared to Marcel Proust and Thomas Mann for the semi-autobiographical work, set with harrowing detail in a Swiss TB sanatorium. The book is now viewed as a modern classic.

GENDER BENDERS

Many female writers have found it expedient to adopt a male pseudonym. The three Brontë sisters, Charlotte (1816–55), Emily (1818–48) and Anne (1820–49), published their respective novels as 'Currer Bell', 'Ellis Bell' and 'Acton Bell'. Another English writer who used the same tactic to ensure her work was taken seriously was George Eliot, born Mary Ann Evans (1819–80). Eliot, whose best-known novels include *Adam Bede* (1859), *The Mill on the Floss* (1860), *Middlemarch* (1872) and *Daniel Deronda* (1876), was encouraged to write by the philosopher and critic George Henry Lewis, with whom she lived for many years.

In France, Amantine Lucile Aurore Dupin (1804–76) elected to call herself 'George Sand'. Leaving her husband, Baron Dudevant, and the family home, Sand launched herself on the

Parisian cultural scene, writing novels that challenged the social norms. An early feminist, she scandalously smoked in public and went about in men's clothes. Free love was high on her agenda and among those with whom she had affairs were playwright Prosper Mérimée (1803–70), poet Alfred de Musset (1810–57) and composer Frédéric Chopin (1810–49). The great Russian writer Ivan Turgenev said of her: 'What a brave man she was, and what a good woman.'

The Danish writer Karen Blixen (1885–1962) employed several pseudonyms in her writing career, the most familiar of which is Isak Dinesen. It was under this name that two of her most famous works were published: the memoir *Out of Africa* (1937), an account of her life in Kenya, and the short story 'Babette's Feast' (1950), both of which were turned into Oscar-winning movies.

J. K. Rowling switched genre and gender with her 2013 crime novel *The Cuckoo's Calling*, which appeared under the name of Robert Galbraith. As the mega-selling author of the Harry Potter books explained: 'I was yearning to go back to the beginning of a writing career in this new genre, to work without hype or expectation and to receive totally unvarnished feedback.' Her secret lasted three months following publication. When news got out that RG was none other than JKR sales of the book soared, climbing from 4,709th in the Amazon sales chart to number one.

WHY 'VOLTAIRE'?

As a child, the French writer and philosopher Voltaire, real name François-Marie Arouet (1694–1778), a giant of the so-called 'Age of Enlightenment', was known within the family as *le petit volontaire* ('determined little fellow') and many think his pen name derives from that. Others favour the explanation that 'Voltaire' is an inversion of 'Airvault', the town in west-central France from which his family originated. Unfortunately, the great man left everyone unenlightened.

DIFFERENT HATS

The former Poet Laureate Cecil Day-Lewis (1904–72), father of actor Daniel Day-Lewis, wrote mystery stories under the name of Nicholas Blake. Early on in his career, the eminent American writer Gore Vidal (1925–2012) produced several detective novels as Edgar Box. Agatha Christie (1890–1976) temporarily turned away from crime to publish, as Mary Westmacott, half a dozen romantic novels.

New York-born Salvatore Albert Lombino (1926–2005) legally changed his name to Evan Hunter and wrote a series of bestselling novels, starting with *The Blackboard Jungle* in 1954. As Ed McBain, he embarked on a parallel (and even more successful) career in crime fiction with a series of police procedural novels and stories about the 87th Precinct, many of which have been adapted for television and cinema.

Few people have heard of Eleanor Hibbert (1906–93) but millions have read the novels of Jean Plaidy, Victoria Holt and Phillipa Carr, just three of the pen names employed by this prolific English author. The Jean Plaidy historical novels tapped into the rich vein of European royalty. As Victoria Holt, Hibbert churned out gothic romances. Family sagas were the speciality of Phillipa Carr. Under her maiden name, Eleanor Burford, she wrote romantic tales for Mills and Boon. In all, Eleanor Hibbert produced more than 200 books, with global sales topping 100 million copies.

Sir Arthur Quiller-Couch (1863–1944), novelist, poet and editor of the first *Oxford Book of English Verse* (1900), had a minimalist approach to pseudonyms. The distinguished man of letters simply called himself 'Q'.

STAYING NEUTRAL

Some writers see benefits in being gender neutral. The publishers of J. K. Rowling's Harry Potter books advised the author to use initials rather than her full name, in order not to put off young male readers. As Joanne Rowling didn't have a middle name, she 'borrowed' the initial K from her grandmother Kathleen.

The British writer Sean Thomas (1963–), son of novelist and poet D. M. Thomas (author of *The White Hotel*, 1981), published three novels under his own name before adopting the pseudonym Tom Knox. Five thrillers later, he changed his nomenclature once again, this time to S. K. Tremayne: in part so he could write fiction from a female perspective.

Another writer who has taken up the gender-neutral option is S. J. Watson (1971–), author of the international bestseller-turned-movie *Before I Go to Sleep* (2011). The thriller is narrated by a female character, who might have had less credibility if seen to have been created by a man. S. J. (Steve) Watson's follow-up novel, *Second Life* (2015), also has a female narrator – though few would now question the author's credentials.

IT'S A FACT!

The Scottish writer A. L. Kennedy (1965–) chose to be known by her initials in homage to her childhood literary heroes, E. Nesbit, J. R. R. Tolkien and C. S. Lewis. For the record, the initials stand for Alison Louise.

IDENTITY UNKNOWN

The real identity of the novelist called B. Traven may never be conclusively established. His best-known novel, one of a dozen that were published, is *The Treasure of the Sierra Madre* (1927), later an Academy Award-winning movie directed by John Huston. Traven has been the subject of numerous investigations by journalists and literary scholars over the years, intrigued by his story – or lack of it. The most popular theory is that he was one Hermann Albert Otto Max Feige, born in Germany *c.*1882. Feige became a political activist, changing his name to Ret Marat along the way, and took part in the failed Communist uprising in Munich in 1919. He escaped execution by fleeing the country and eventually ended up in Mexico, where he began to write as B. Traven, though neither his publishers nor anyone else knowingly had face-to-face contact with him.

During the filming of *The Treasure of the Sierra Madre* in 1948, someone calling himself Hal Croves arrived on the set and claimed to be Traven's agent. Many believed it was Traven himself (though interestingly, John Huston, who had had a lengthy correspondence with the writer, thought otherwise). When Croves died in Mexico in 1969, his widow revealed that he and Traven and Ret Marat had been one and the same, although other information she supplied has since been disputed.

B. Traven, whoever he was, once wrote: 'The biography of a creative man is completely unimportant.'

ANGLICISED VERSION

Joseph Conrad (1857–1924) is one of the most influential British novelists of the twentieth century, yet he didn't speak English until he was nineteen years old. Born to Polish parents in what is now Ukraine, his real name was Józef Teodor Konrad Korzeniowski. He was an avid reader in both Polish and French as a child, but only began to speak English after signing up with the British Merchant Navy. He worked at sea for the next fifteen years, eventually rising to the rank of captain. After the successful publication of his first novel, *Almayer's Folly* (1895), Conrad came ashore for good and settled in England. Among his best known novels are *An Outcast of the Islands* (1896), *Lord Jim* (1900), *Nostromo* (1904) and *The Secret Agent* (1907). His short story 'Heart of Darkness' was the basis for Francis Ford Coppola's 1979 film *Apocalypse Now*.

TWO FOR ONE

Magnus Flyte is the pseudonym of two American writers, Meg Howrey, who has also published novels under her own name, and Christina Lynch, a television writer and journalist. The collaborators met at a writers' retreat, where they conjured up their literary alias. Two 'Magnus Flyte' mysteries were published in quick succession: *City of Dark Magic* (2012) and *City of Lost Dreams* (2013).

One of the most successful literary collaborations goes under the name of Nicci French. The bestselling author of some twenty thrillers (the most recent series featuring investigative psychotherapist Frieda Klein) is in fact the English husband-and-wife team, Nicci Gerrard (1958–) and Sean French (1959–). Both are former journalists and both have independently written other books under their own names. Sean French is the son of the former film critic Philip French (1933–2015).

In 1928, two American cousins entered the novel they wrote together for a writing contest sponsored by *McClure's Magazine* for the best 'first mystery novel'. In order to ensure impartiality, contestants were required to employ a pseudonym and the two writers decided on Ellery Queen, the name of the detective in their story. They won the competition and launched the career of one of America's most famous fictional detectives, who is in effect also the author of the books. The names of the two writers were Frederic Dannay (1905–82) and Manfred B. Lee (1905–71), though these themselves were pseudonyms, their real names being Daniel Nathan and Emanuel Benjamin Lepofsky. Together they wrote more than thirty Ellery Queen novels and story collections spanning forty-two years. Dannay and Lee also produced four novels under the pen name Barnaby Ross, featuring an ex-thespian detective theatrically named Drury Lane.

NAMES BEHIND THE NAMES

Pen name	Real name
Molière	Jean-Baptiste Poquelin (1622–73)
Susan Coolidge	Sarah Chauncey Woolsey (1835–1905)
Mark Twain	Samuel Langhorne Clemens (1835–1910)
Saki	Hector Hugh Munro (1870–1916)
Antonia White	Eirine Botting (1899–1980)

Flann O'Brien	Brian O'Nolan (1911–66)
Ellis Peters	Edith Mary Pargeter (1913–95)
Patrick O'Brian	Richard Patrick Russ (1914–2000)
Anthony Burgess	John Wilson (1917–93)
Iceberg Slim	Robert Beck (1918–92)
Richard Gordon	Gordon Stanley Ostlere (1921–2017)
Fay Weldon	Franklin Birkinshaw (1931–)
Anne Rice	Howard Allen Frances O'Brien (1941–)

DEFINING DICTIONARIES

In 1746, Samuel Johnson (1709–84) was commissioned by a group of London booksellers to compile a dictionary, the first of its kind in English. Born in Lichfield, in Warwickshire, Johnson had started working life as a schoolmaster, but in 1737 he moved to London accompanied by his wife, twenty years his senior, and one of his pupils, later to become the celebrated actor David Garrick, and quickly made his mark in literary circles. *A Dictionary of the English Language* (1755) took just over eight years to complete. Johnson employed six assistants, though the bulk of the work he did himself (a comparable French dictionary had taken half a century to compile with the input of forty scholars). 'Johnson's Dictionary', as it is often called, contains over 40,000 words, the definitions of which are enhanced by some 114,000 quotations drawn from every field of literature and learning. Occasionally, Johnson allowed a lighter note to creep into his explanatory text, as in: *lexicographer*: 'a writer of dictionaries, a harmless drudge.' His work remained unrivalled until the publication of the more substantial *Oxford English Dictionary* in 1858.

The American lexicographer and grammarian Noah Webster (1758–1843) published his famous dictionary in 1828. *An American Dictionary of the English Language* took twenty-eight years to compile and contained 70,000 words, 12,000 of which were listed in a dictionary for the first time. In order to carry out his formidable task, Webster acquired a working knowledge of twenty-six languages, including Hebrew, Latin, Greek, Russian, Sanskrit and Old English. He set out to simplify the spelling of certain words, introducing American-English versions of colour (color), waggon (wagon), centre (center) and musick (music). Webster's pedantry in linguistic matters gave rise to an apocryphal story. As the tale goes, he was caught by his wife kissing a chambermaid. 'Why Noah,' she said, 'I'm surprised.' 'Madame,' the lexicographer corrected her, adopting the correct usage of the time, '*You* are astonished; *I* am *surprised*.'

IT'S A FACT!

According to the *Guinness World Records*, China's *Xinhua Dictionary* is the most popular lexicon in the world. First published in 1953, its global sales to date are around 570 million copies.

CHILDREN'S CLASSICS

‘*A children's story that can only be enjoyed by children is not a good children's story in the slightest.*’

C. S. LEWIS (1898–1963)

There were few books specifically created for children before the middle of the eighteenth century. A bookseller named Thomas Boreman, who had a stall near the Guildhall in London, is thought to be the first specialist publisher of children's books. In 1730, he published *A Description of Three Hundred Animals*, following it up six years later with *A Description of a Great Variety of Animals and Vegetables*. It wasn't yet the age of the snappy title.

THE 'FATHER OF CHILDREN'S LITERATURE'

Another publisher, John Newbery (1713–67), was the first to recognise and seriously develop the new genre. He produced books designed for a young readership, with distinctively small formats and attractive illustrations. His first book appeared in 1744: *A Little Pretty Pocket-Book, intended for the Amusement of Little Master Tommy and Pretty Miss Polly with Two Letters from Jack the Giant Killer.* The book was cannily marketed with 'freebies' – a ball for boys, a pincushion for girls – and comprised simple rhymes for each letter of the alphabet.

Newbery, who helped finance his publishing activities by selling patent medicines, later produced a bestseller in *The History of Little Goody Two-Shoes* (1765), popularising the phrase for generations to come. No author was credited, but some scholars have pinned the work on the poet and playwright Oliver Goldsmith (1730–74). A series of non-fiction books charting recent developments in the world of science was written under the name 'Tom Telescope', and ran into many editions. John Newbery's contribution to children's literature is remembered today in the form of the Newbery Medal, awarded annually for the best children's book by an American author.

TELLING TALES

The brothers Grimm, Jacob (1785–1863) and Wilhelm (1786–1859), were German folklorists and linguists, famous for the collaborative work popularly known as *Grimms' Fairy-Tales*. The first edition was published in 1812. Over the next forty-five years a further six editions were produced, revising and enlarging the collection and editing out elements deemed unsuitable for children. The brothers went out into the field (sometimes literally) to gather their material, transcribing traditional tales told to them by peasants and others. Among the legendary stories gleaned were those of 'Snow White', 'Sleeping Beauty', 'Little Red Riding Hood', 'Tom Thumb', and 'Hansel and Gretel'.

Round about the same time, a Danish writer was telling stories of his own. Hans Christian Andersen (1805–75) was a prolific playwright, novelist and poet, though he is principally known now for the enchanting fairy tales that have captivated generations of children – and not a few adults. The stories, 168 in all, include 'The Red Shoes', 'The Ugly Duckling', 'The Emperor's New Clothes' and 'The Little Mermaid'. Big on moral virtues and laced with words of wisdom, these timeless tales have inspired ballets, films and songs. During a visit to England, Andersen met Charles Dickens and the two carried on a cordial relationship, largely at arm's length until Andersen was invited in 1857 to stay for a few days at Gad's Hill, the Dickens' family home. The visitor ('a bony bore' in the words of Dickens' daughter Kate) hung around for five weeks, exhausting the patience of his host. It proved a less than fairy-tale ending to their friendship.

DARK SIDE

Louisa May Alcott (1832–88), whose novels *Little Women* (1868), *Little Men* (1871) and *Jo's Boys* (1886) continue to command a young readership, was a manic-depressive who suffered from nightmares and hallucinations. She was forced to work from an early age in order to support her financially stricken family. Several times she contemplated suicide. She was a nurse during the American Civil War, but contracted typhoid and then mercury poisoning from the medication she received, an experience which permanently undermined her physique. A social reformer who fought for the abolition of slavery and for women's rights, Alcott never married, leaving that to the characters in her books.

CLASSIC TITLES

Many enduring classics emerged during the nineteenth century. Charles Kingsley (1819–75), clergyman and novelist, wrote the historical adventure *Westward Ho!* (1855) and the moralistic fantasy *The Water Babies* (1863), in which a young chimney sweep named Tom falls into the river and is transformed into a do-gooding water sprite. *Tom Brown's Schooldays* (1857) by Thomas Hughes (1822–96) portrays the ups and downs of life at an English public school – in this case Rugby – and introduced the sixth-form bully Flashman; resurrected for an adult readership a century later in a series of comic adventure novels by George MacDonald Fraser (1925–2008).

The Scottish author Robert Louis Stevenson (1850–94) wrote *Treasure Island* (1883) and *Kidnapped* (1886), two rip-roaring adventure stories that like many children's books down the years are relished by adults as well. Those who cannot spare the time to read *Kidnapped* might just settle for its subtitle: *Being the Memoirs of the Adventures of David Balfour in the Year 1751; How he was Kidnapped and Cast Away, His Suffering on a Desert Isle; His Journey in the Wild Highlands; His Acquaintance with Alan Breck Stewart and Other Notorious Highland Jacobites; With all that he Suffered at the Hands of his Uncle, Ebenezer Balfour of Shaws, Falsely So Called. Written by Himself and Now Set Forth by Robert Louis Stevenson.*

The Indian-born Rudyard Kipling (1865–1936) imaginatively returned to his sub-continental roots for *The Jungle Book* (1894), in which the two-legged infant Mowgli is raised by the four-legged Mother Wolf.

In America, Louisa May Alcott (1832–88) and Mark Twain (1835–1910) produced a clutch of classics between them. Alcott's saga about the March family's 'little women' extended to three novels. The author herself was one of four sisters (as in the books) and the setting for the stories owes much to Alcott's family home in Massachusetts. Jo March, the tomboyish and literary member of the quartet, represents the author, at least at heart. Mark Twain drew on his own youthful experiences in Hannibal, Missouri (called St Petersburg in the book) for *The Adventures of Tom Sawyer* (1876). Tom's exploits on the banks of the mighty Mississippi make lively reading, but it is the book's more serious 'sequel', *The Adventures of Huckleberry Finn* (1884), in which Tom's boon companion from the first novel is the eponymous hero, that is Twain's masterpiece.

In Switzerland, the hills were alive with the sound of Heidi, the eponymous heroine of Johanna Spyri's (1827–1901) novel about a young girl who lives with her grandfather in the Alps. Published in 1881, *Heidi* is one of the most read children's books of all time. An earlier blockbuster from the same country is *The Swiss Family Robinson* (1812) by Johann David Wyss (1743–1818), a story about a family shipwrecked on route to Australia – a familial version of *Robinson Crusoe*.

ILLUSTRATING ALICE

Lewis Carroll contemplated illustrating *Alice's Adventures in Wonderland* (1865) himself, but was persuaded to seek the services of a professional artist. Like most Victorian gentlemen, he was a regular reader of *Punch* magazine and familiar with the work of its chief political cartoonist (later Sir) John Tenniel. He chose Tenniel to illustrate the book and, following its success, the sequel: *Through the Looking-Glass, and What Alice Found There* (1871). Since then more than seventy other illustrators have visually interpreted one or both of the Alice texts. Among the more distinguished artists are Arthur Rackham (1907), Mabel Lucie Attwell (1910), Mervyn Peake (1946), Ralph Steadman (1967/72), Salvador Dalì (1969), Helen Oxenbury (1999/2005), Peter Blake (2004), Michael Foreman (2004) and Yayoi Kusama (2012).

PET SUBJECT

A keen student of botany and zoology and a gifted artist and storyteller, Beatrix Potter (1866–1943) created some of the most popular tales ever for young children. However, her literary endeavours got off to an uncertain start. Her first work, *The Tale of Peter Rabbit*, inspired by her pet bunny of that name, was turned down by several publishers who were approached on the author's behalf by her friend and local vicar, Canon Rawnsley. It didn't help that the well-meaning clergyman substituted his own long-winded verse for Potter's succinct prose.

Meeting with no success, the resourceful author decided to have the book published privately. An edition of 250 copies was produced, with black and white illustrations and the original words restored; one copy was bought by the writer Arthur Conan Doyle. When the London publishers Frederick Warne & Co, who had previously declined the book, saw the printed version, they had a change of heart – provided the author supplied colour illustrations and stuck to her own text. The new colourful version of *The Tale of Peter Rabbit* was published in 1902. Peter, who died shortly after the story's first monochrome appearance, was one of Beatrix Potter's two pet rabbits. The other is immortalised in *The Tale of Benjamin Bunny* (1904).

E. B. White (1899–1985), author of two of the most successful children's stories of the twentieth century, *Stuart Little* (1945) and *Charlotte's Web* (1952), wrote for *The New Yorker* magazine for nearly sixty years and was a critically acclaimed essayist and literary stylist.

INSPIRATIONAL SONS

Kenneth Grahame (1859–1932) took early retirement from his post as Secretary of the Bank of England in 1908, the year in which his most famous work, *The Wind in the Willows*, was published. The Edinburgh-born author had produced several children's stories whilst still employed at the bank, but his new book was to eclipse them all. On his retirement, Grahame moved his family to the Thames-side village of Pangbourne in Berkshire, near where he had spent his childhood. The river and its wildlife provided the background to the bedtime stories the author told his only son Alistair, with some of the animals transformed into junior fiction's most celebrated quartet: Mole, Ratty, Badger and Toad.

A. A. Milne (1882–1956) was an established playwright and assistant editor of *Punch* magazine before he produced his first book for children. In 1924, four years after the birth of his son Christopher Robin, Milne published a collection of children's poetry, *When We Were Very Young*. This was followed in 1926 by *Winnie-the-Pooh*, both books illustrated by the *Punch* cartoonist E. H. Shepard (1879–1976). The slow-witted, sweet-toothed Pooh is named after Christopher Robin's own teddy bear (a first-birthday present) and is joined in the book by some of his other toys: Eeyore, Piglet and Kanga. *The House at Pooh Corner* (1928) sees the introduction of another of Christopher's playmates, the bouncing tiger Tigger. The original toy animals are on permanent display in the New York Public Library, a long way from their fictional habitat of Hundred Acre Wood.

The creative paths of the two authors merged in 1929, with Milne's dramatisation of Grahame's bestselling book. The rumbustious *Toad of Toad Hall* was set to run and run.

IT'S A FACT!

Roald Dahl's first children's book, *The Gremlins*, was published in 1943 while the author was serving in Washington D.C. (see chapter The Spying Game, page 147). The book – about gremlins sabotaging British aircraft during the war – was originally commissioned by Walt Disney for an animated film that was never made. It would be another eighteen years before Dahl published a second children's story: *James and the Giant Peach* (1961).

QUEEN B

Estimates of exactly how many children's books Enid Blyton (1897–1968) wrote range between 700 and 800. The first, published in 1922, was a slim volume of poetry entitled *Child Whispers*. This was followed three years later by *The Enid Blyton Book of Bunnies*, after which she launched her long-running weekly magazine *Sunny Stories for Little Folks*. In 1927, she acquired her first typewriter, which enabled her to step up the production rate. Her first bestseller was *Letters from Bobs* (1933) – 'Bobs' was a dog – which sold 10,000 copies in the first week. The Famous Five made their debut in 1942 in *Five on a Treasure Island*. Two years later another hugely popular series got underway with *The Island of Adventure*. For younger readers, Noddy and Big-Ears teamed up in Toyland (in 1949) and over the next twenty years would feature in upwards of 150 books. Rumours appeared in print that the author employed ghost writers to maintain her prolific output, prompting her to take legal action to protect her reputation.

Enid Blyton's success has not come without criticism. There have been accusations of racism, sexism and xenophobia in her work. Her characters have been dismissed as too middle-class, her use of language too limited. Some libraries have gone as far as banning her books. But none of this seems to have dented her popularity among the public. She continues to be one of the world's bestselling children's authors, with sales in excess of 500 million copies. In the UK alone, it is estimated that an Enid Blyton book is sold every single minute.

IT'S A FACT!

At the end of E. Nesbit's much-loved novel *The Railway Children* (1906), Bobbie (Roberta) rushes into the arms of her father, restored to the family after having been falsely imprisoned, with the touching cry: 'Oh! My Daddy, My Daddy!' The author's own father died before her fourth birthday.

THROUGH THE WARDROBE

According to C. S. Lewis (1898–1963), the idea for the first of his Narnia stories, *The Lion, the Witch and the Wardrobe*, sprang from a mental picture of a 'faun carrying an umbrella and parcels in a snowy wood'. He never forgot the image, which had sprung to mind when he was in his teens, and some twenty-five years later decided to do something about it.

The first novel in the seven-book series was published in 1950. Thereafter, the books appeared at the rate of one a year, culminating in *The Last Battle* (1956). The Narnia series has been translated into nearly fifty languages, with total sales of over 100 million copies. The Belfast-born Lewis was a distinguished literary scholar and a deeply religious man, writing several books on Christian ethics. He also wrote a number of novels for adults, including a sci-fi series known as *The Space Trilogy* (1938–45). As for the name 'Narnia', the author claimed it came from Narni, a small town in Italy between Rome and Assisi, which he had randomly spotted on a map and which struck a chord. Just like that inspirational image.

SOME WIZARD FACTS ABOUT HARRY POTTER

- *Harry Potter and the Philosopher's Stone* (1997), the first book in the series, has been translated into more than seventy languages, including Latin and ancient Greek.
- The name 'Joanne Rowling' appears in small type on the copyright page of the very first edition, of which just 500 copies were printed.
- Creating the cover illustration for the original UK edition of *Harry Potter and the Philosopher's Stone* was artist Thomas Taylor's first professional commission.
- For the six months following publication of her first book, and until the author's true identity was revealed during a television interview, all fan mail addressed to J. K. Rowling began 'Dear Sir'.
- Professor Dumbledore's name is an old English word for 'bumblebee'. J. K. Rowling called him that because she imagined him always humming to himself.

- The driver and conductor of the Knight Bus in *Harry Potter and the Prisoner of Azkaban* (1999), Stan Shunpike and Ernie Prang, are in part named after JKR's grandfathers, Stanley and Ernest.
- The Dementors, the dark creatures that feed off human happiness, were inspired by JKR's own struggles with depression following the death of her mother.
- The initial print run for *Harry Potter and the Deathly Hallows* (2007) was 12 million copies, the largest-ever first printing of a book.
- In 2007, a sixteen-year-old boy was arrested in France for publishing online an unauthorised French version of *Harry Potter and the Deathly Hallows*, which he had translated himself.
- JKR's advance for the first Harry Potter book was £2,500. It is estimated that her total earnings since then are in excess of $1 billion.

TEENAGE ANGST

The American writer Judy Blume (1938–) helped create a new market for young adult fiction with novels that dealt with hitherto taboo subjects such as puberty, sex and death. In *Are You There God? It's Me, Margaret* (1970), a twelve-year-old girl, half-Jewish, half-Catholic, searches for a meaningful religious identity whilst facing up to less spiritual challenges like buying a first bra. *Blubber* (1974) centres on the bullying of a vulnerable overweight schoolgirl; while *Forever* (1975) is a no-holds-barred exploration of teenage sexuality. Blume's work has attracted controversy in some quarters and at times has been censored. But to her millions of teen readers she has provided enlightenment and reassurance, and plenty of entertainment.

Another successful exponent of the teenage novel is the English writer Anne Fine (1947–), author of more than fifty books and former Children's Laureate. Her best-known work in the genre is *Madame Doubtfire* (1987), a funny and perceptive story about children coping with the domestic upheaval that follows their parents' divorce. The title was changed to *Mrs Doubtfire* for the 1993 Hollywood film.

Divorce, adoption and mental illness are some of the themes to be found in the teenage fiction of Jacqueline Wilson (1945–), though it is only fair to add that she has written about more cheerful topics as well. The Bath-born author has more than a hundred titles to her name (many of them adapted for television), including the popular *Tracy Beaker* series about an unhappy and disruptive ten-year-old who lives in a care home; the self-explanatory *Girls in Love* (1997) which has spawned three sequels; and *Vicky Angel* (2000), a young girl's struggle to come to terms with the death of her best friend.

TEN CLASSIC PICTURE BOOKS

Madeline (1939)	Ludwig Bemelmans
The Cat in the Hat (1957)	Dr Seuss
Where the Wild Things Are (1963)	Maurice Sendak
The Tiger Who Came to Tea (1968)	Judith Kerr
The Very Hungry Caterpillar (1969)	Eric Carle
The Snowman (1978)	Raymond Briggs
Where's Spot? (1980)	Eric Hill
The Jolly Postman (1986)	Janet and Allan Ahlberg
We're Going on a Bear Hunt (1989)	Michael Rosen and Helen Oxenbury
The Gruffalo (1999)	Julia Donaldson and Axel Scheffler

BESTSELLING PHENOMENA

*❛I never set out to do this – getting to
No. 1 in the* New York Times *bestseller
list wasn't even a pipe dream.❜*

E. L. JAMES

Some bestsellers are predictable: for example, every *Harry Potter* sequel. John le Carré's spy novels have routinely entered the bestseller charts on both sides of the Atlantic, with three in succession reaching the top spot in America. The latest offering cooked up by one of television's culinary superstars is bound to simmer for weeks in the Top Ten; and the *Wisden Cricketers' Almanack* (155 not out) annually takes its place in the lists, at least in the UK.

Other bestsellers turn up unexpectedly, however. The exquisitely illustrated *Nature Notes for 1906* by a little known British artist and teacher, Edith Holden (1871–1920), was posthumously published in facsimile form as *The Country Diary of an Edwardian Lady* in 1977 and proved an enormous success, especially as a gift. Dava Sobel's *Longitude* (1995), the story behind the eighteenth-century invention of the marine chronometer, was an unlikely subject for an international bestseller. Another science book to make it big is Stephen Hawking's *A Brief History of Time* (1988), which has sold more than 10 million copies and remained on *The Sunday Times* bestseller list for a record 250 weeks.

In the USA 8.3 million copies of *Harry Potter and the Deathly Hallows* (2007) were sold in the first twenty-four hours of its publication, making it the fastest-selling book ever.

CRACKING THE CODE

One of the biggest-selling fiction titles this century has been Dan Brown's *The Da Vinci Code* (2004), combining elements of the traditional detective story with the pacy violence of a modern thriller, with some questionable academic and religious theorising thrown in. The book attracted strong criticism, with Salman Rushdie and Stephen King among the literary critics who publicly ridiculed the plot and the banality of the writing (it hasn't gone unnoticed that Dan Brown is a former teacher of English). Experts have pointed to a host of historical inaccuracies in the book, and religious groups have been offended by the author's depiction of aspects of the Christian faith. None of this can be said to have slowed down sales, though charity shops have reported copies of *The Da Vinci Code* being donated at the rate of one a week – which suggests few people plan to read it twice.

GOLD RUSH

The American writer Zane Grey (1872–1939) pioneered the western genre. Born Pearl Zane Grey in Zanesville, Ohio, he began his professional life as a dentist in New York, but soon caught the writing bug. He would extract teeth by day and compose stories by night, initially with little success. His first novel was self-published, but he gradually found a market for his work and hit the jackpot in 1912 with *Riders of the Purple Sage*, a runaway bestseller and one of the best known westerns of all time. Grey went on to write over sixty books with a combined sales in his lifetime of 13 million copies – a figure that has more than doubled since then. For almost a decade he was never out of the bestseller lists, though nowadays much of his work is out of print. His novels and short stories have been the basis for more than 100 films.

COSTLY REJECTIONS

Publishing history is littered with missed opportunities. R. D. Blackmore's (1825–1900) historical romance *Lorna Doone* (1869) was rejected by eighteen publishers before becoming a major classic. The manuscript of George Orwell's allegorical tale *Animal Farm* (1945) was politely returned by several publishers on both sides of the Atlantic, including his incumbent one, before being accepted elsewhere. The Norwegian adventurer Thor Heyerdahl's (1914–2002) account of crossing the Pacific on a raft, *Kon-Tiki* (1950), was found insufficiently interesting by twenty US publishing houses. Millions of copies have since been sold. Another multimillion seller that slipped through several nets was *Jonathan Livingstone Seagull* (1970), Richard Bach's fabled flight to spiritual freedom.

Richard Adams' first novel *Watership Down* (1972) was rejected by a number of hardback publishers in London (one on the grounds that no one would buy a book whose hero was a male rabbit called Hazel). The book was taken on by a one-man publishing band, Rex Collings, and went on to collect the Carnegie Medal and Guardian Prize, both prestigious awards for children's books. Before long Hazel and his bunny buddies were household names.

But the biggest missed opportunity of them all was J. K. Rowling's *Harry Potter and the Philosopher's Stone*. Her agent sent the manuscript of her first novel to no fewer than twelve publishers, before it was accepted by Bloomsbury – largely on the say so of the company chairman's eight-year-old daughter Alice (a resonant name in children's literature) who had enthusiastically read a sample chapter. In a neat coda to this story, the first publisher to turn down *Harry Potter* also rejected *The Cuckoo's Calling* (2013), Rowling's debut crime novel submitted pseudonymously as Robert Galbraith. Some people never learn.

Still, given the success of so many books and writers, and the countless works of distinction that would never have made it into print were it not for enterprising editors, publishers can justifiably claim to have got far more right than wrong.

MR BESTSELLER

When seven-year-old Adam Hargreaves asked his father what a tickle looked like, it was the start of what would become a multimillion-pound publishing story. In response to his son's casual enquiry, father Roger, creative director of a London advertising agency, sketched his impressions on paper. A year later, in 1971, an enhanced version in the guise of *Mr. Tickle* was published, along with five other Mr. Men books. Little Miss, a companion series, followed almost ten years to the day.

Since Roger Hargreaves' death in 1988, at the age of fifty-three, Adam has taken on the authorial mantle, creating new characters for both series: among them Mr. Cool and Mr. Rude, Little Miss Scary and Little Miss Princess. There are now some ninety titles across the two series, with global sales of over 250 million copies. With sales figures like that, what author wouldn't be tickled?

IF AT FIRST YOU DON'T SUCCEED

Aspiring writers should be encouraged by the example of the British author John Creasey (1908–73) who published close to 600 books in his career, employing twenty-eight pseudonyms in the process. He is best known for his crime novels, but he also wrote science fiction, westerns and, as 'Margaret Cooke' (his first wife's name), several romantic stories. Much of his crime fiction was adapted for cinema and television, with characters like Inspector Gideon of Scotland Yard, the Toff (a.k.a. the Hon. Richard Rollinson) and the Baron (part antiques dealer, part secret agent) becoming familiar to millions of viewers as well as readers.

Creasey was born into a working-class family in Southfields, Surrey, the seventh of nine children. His first book was published when he was twenty-two; five years later he became a full-time writer. But it wasn't all plain sailing. During these early years, Creasey received a total of 743 rejection slips, a collective response that didn't deter him; and just as well, because at his peak, his annual sales totalled around 2.5 million copies. In 1953, the redoubtable Creasey founded the Crime Writers' Association, becoming its first chairman. He also launched a political party, married four times and still managed to write between 7,000 and 10,000 words a day. What more encouragement do you need?

IT'S A FACT!

The American poet E. E. Cummings (1884–1962) self-published a book of his poetry in 1935. The dedication began: 'No thanks to...' after which Cummings listed the fifteen publishing houses that had previously turned down his manuscript.

FIFTY SHADES

If E. L. James, real name Erika Mitchell (1963–), had opted for a more conventional approach to getting her first book published, she might not have succeeded. Inspired by Stephanie Meyer's vampire romance series *Twilight* (another bestselling phenomenon), James wrote a story called *Master of the Universe*, which she posted episodically on a fan-fiction website, using the pseudonym 'Snowqueen's Icedragon'. Concerns about the sexual content prompted James to switch the material to her own website, where the readership continued to build. Sometime later she reconfigured the work as a trilogy, changing the title and the names of the principal characters. A viral publisher in Australia took on the project and, in May 2011, released the first part of the trilogy – *Fifty Shades of Grey* – as an eBook and print-on-demand paperback. The second instalment, *Fifty Shades Darker*, appeared four months later, followed in January 2012 by

Fifty Shades Freed. The success of the viral campaign led to the sale of conventional publishing rights and, at long last, *Fifty Shades* made its way into bookshops.

The books have topped bestseller lists around the world, with global sales of well over 125 million copies. The sexual saga has been translated into more than fifty languages, among them Albanian, Russian and Vietnamese. Significantly, the trilogy's success has been built on word-of-mouth recommendation, bypassing the critics who have almost universally panned the books. Not that that is likely to concern E. L. James, who might justifiably claim to know more about what turns on her readers.

IT'S A FACT!

The bestselling novel of all time is thought to be *Don Quixote* (1605) by Miguel de Cervantes, with sales of around 500 million, though for obvious reasons there are no accurate figures to support the claim. The leading British contender, with 200 million copies to its name, is *A Tale of Two Cities* (1859) by Charles Dickens.

SETTING RECORDS

During the course of a shooting party in County Wexford, Ireland, an argument developed over which was the fastest game bird in Europe. Unable to find the answer in any reference book, one of those involved, the then managing director of Guinness Brewery, decided to sponsor a publication that would resolve such dilemmas. The sporting twins, Ross (1925–75) and Norris (1925–2004) McWhirter, journalists and avid collectors of facts, were commissioned to produce it. Thus was born *The Guinness Book of Records.*

The first edition was published in August 1955, with a print run of 50,000 copies. The slim volume in a plain green cover contained just one full-colour illustration in its 198 pages. By Christmas it had become the UK's No. 1 bestselling non-fiction title. The book was launched in America the following year with similar success. Since then the book has become an institution, extending its franchise into television series and museums, and breaking records of its own. Published in 100 countries, with sales approaching 140 million, it is officially the world's bestselling non-fiction copyrighted book of all time (the Bible and the Qur'an, of course, are not copyrighted). In 1999, the title was changed to *Guinness World Records*. As for that pertinent question regarding the speediest game bird: the answer is, the plover.

TEN FICTION WRITERS WITH SALES IN THE STRATOSPHERE

Author	Sample title
Agatha Christie (1890–1976)	*And Then There Were None* (1939)
Barbara Cartland (1901–2000)	*The Wicked Marquis* (1973)
Danielle Steel (1947–)	*The Long Road Home* (1998)
James Patterson (1947–)	*Along Came a Spider* (1993)
Harold Robbins (1916–97)	*The Carpetbaggers* (1961)
Georges Simenon (1903–89)	*Maigret's First Case* (1948)
Sidney Sheldon (1917–2007)	*Rage of Angels* (1980)
Stephen King (1947–)	*Carrie* (1974)
Dean Koontz (1945–)	*Watchers* (2003)
Jeffrey Archer (1940–)	*Kane and Abel* (1979)

CODA

This is a true story. In a small community in the remote, arid north-east of Brazil lives twelve-year-old Ricardo Oliveira Costa. His greatest passion is reading, his proudest possessions books. From the age of seven, Ricardo dreamt of building a library. When a small, dusty plot of land next to his family's modest home came up for sale, Ricardo decided to do something about it. A talented young artist, he painted pictures to sell to anyone who would buy them. After four years of artistic endeavour he had raised enough money to purchase the land.

The next challenge was to acquire books for his dream library. His mother bought him a new suit and a purple suitcase on wheels. Thus formally attired, Ricardo went from door to door asking people to donate books for his cause. Time and again he filled the suitcase, amassing over 5,000 volumes. They called him the 'boy of books'. He rode on horseback to neighbouring settlements to read to children who couldn't themselves read. 'A child who doesn't read,' he told them, 'is like a plane with no wings: it won't take off.'

Word of Ricardo's literary crusade spread throughout Brazil and beyond. An international sponsor came up with money to complete the project. A simple one-storey building was erected and shelving (quickly filled) installed. In 2017, in front of a grateful and admiring community, Ricardo cut the red ribbon that opened his brand new library. One boy's remarkable story – and all for the love of books.

RESOURCES

MAGAZINES

The Times Literary Supplement (weekly)
Reviews, interviews, poetry, extracts from new fiction.
www.the-tls.co.uk

London Review of Books (fortnightly)
Literary essays, book reviews, new poetry.
www.lrb.co.uk

The Reader (quarterly)
Showcases new fiction and poetry as well as established works.
www.thereader.org.uk

Writing Magazine (monthly)
For aspiring writers: interviews, masterclasses, publishing opportunities.
www.warnersgroup.uk/creative-leisure/writing-magazine

LIBRARIES

The British Library
96 Euston Rd, London NW1 2DB
UK's national library.
www.bl.uk

Chetham's Library
Long Millgate, Manchester M3 1SB
Oldest public library in the English-speaking world.
library.chethams.com

Bodleian Library
Broad St, Oxford OX1 3BG
Second only in size to the British Library.
www.bodleian.ox.ac.uk

The Chained Library
Hereford Cathedral
The eighth-century *Hereford Gospels* are among the volumes securely chained up.
www.herefordcathedral.org/chained-library

Innerpeffray Library
Innerpeffray, Crieff PH7 3RF
Scotland's first lending library.
www.innerpeffraylibrary.co.uk

LITERARY FESTIVALS

Hay
Hay-on-Wye, Wales
www.hayfestival.com

Port Eliot
St Germans, Cornwall
www.porteliotfestival.com

Stoke Newington
Stoke Newington, London N16
www.stokenewingtonliteraryfestival.com

Aldeburgh
Aldeburgh, Suffolk
www.aldeburghbookshop.co.uk/page/the-aldeburgh-literary-festival

Harrogate
Harrogate, North Yorkshire
www.harrogate-festival.org.uk

Edinburgh
Edinburgh, Scotland
www.edbookfest.co.uk

WRITERS' HOMES

The Brontës
Brontë Parsonage, Haworth, West Yorkshire
www.bronte.org.uk

Charles Dickens
48 Doughty Street, London WC1
www.dickensmuseum.com

Rudyard Kipling
Bateman's, Burwash, East Sussex
www.nationaltrust.org.uk/batemans

Henry James
Lamb House, Rye, East Sussex
www.nationaltrust.org.uk/lamb-house

Dr Samuel Johnson
17 Gough Square, London EC4
www.drjohnsonshouse.org

Beatrix Potter
Hill Top, Near Sawrey, Cumbria
www.nationaltrust.org.uk/hill-top

Sir Walter Scott
Abbotsford House, Melrose, Scottish Borders
www.scottsabbotsford.co.uk

George Bernard Shaw
Shaw's Corner, Ayot St Lawrence, Welwyn, Herts
www.nationaltrust.org.uk/shaws-corner

Dylan Thomas
Dylan Thomas Boathouse, Laugharne, Carmarthenshire
www.dylanthomasboathouse.com

William Wordsworth
Dove Cottage, Grasmere, Cumbria
www.wordsworth.org.uk

If you're interested in finding out more about our books,
find us on Facebook at **Summersdale Publishers** and
follow us on Twitter at **@Summersdale**.

www.summersdale.com